MW00945295

SOFTWARE
TEST DESIGN
THROUGH BEHAVIORAL MODELING

SHEL PRINCE

ISBN: TBA 1-4392-1227-9

ISBN-13: 9781439212271

Visit www.booksurge.com to order additional copies.

DEDICATION:

To my wife
NANCY

To our daughters
MELISSA, MICHELLE, ANDREA, and HEATHER

To our son
CHRISTOPHER

To our grandchildren
VINCENT, HANNAH, TRISTAN, HAILEY, and GRACE &
Sara

ACKNOWLEDGMENTS:

I have met many people along the way who either helped shape my ideas or helped me to clarify my thinking and I am grateful to all of them. There are three people I would like to mention explicitly. Ed Kit's excellent book, <u>Software Testing in the Real World</u>, offers insights into testing and verification. Greg Pope and I have had many conversations about testing and quality over the years and I have been long impressed with his ideas. Lisa Pappas edited the first version of this book. I have added sections since that time, and any errors introduced by me are not a reflection of her fine work.

TABLE OF CONTENTS

FIGURES

INTRODUCTION

WHAT'S THE PROBLEM?

A growing number of books on testing are available today. They cover many aspects of the profession, but, sadly, most lack a detailed description of how to design a good set of test cases or test suite. A good test suite will help to solve the most pressing problems we see in testing. What are these problems? There are three.

Problem 1: Testing Takes Too Long

From the perspective of the project manager, testing takes too long. The length of a test is primarily dependent on two basic factors: the number of test cases and the quality of the article under test. While there is not much the test engineer can do about the initial quality of the article under test, the number of test cases is under his or her direct control. (As an aside, there actually is something the test engineer can do about the initial quality—we will see a bit later.) Good test design will determine the minimum necessary number of test cases needed to fully test the article. Without good test design, there are usually many redundant test cases—test cases that do not add any additional information.

If testing is taking too long, then two things result. First, the cost of the test is higher—sometimes much higher—than it needs to be. Second, the longer the test, the longer the users have to wait for the functions and services provided by the product; this results in both unhappy users and possibly additional cost as well.

Problem 2: Testing Misses Too Many Bugs

We have all seen situations where applications are deployed with too many bugs. Notice the "too many" part. It is unrealistic to hope that every single bug has been squashed by the testing process, but too much is too much.

Why are bugs missed? Two reasons. The most likely reason is that the test design did not specify all the needed tests. This is despite the fact that there are more tests than are needed. There is a LOT of redundancy out there! The other reason, although we hate to admit it, is that the end date arrived, and the article was deployed, even though testing was not complete. Other than flailing and moaning, there really isn't much a test engineer can do about this second issue. We will focus on the first. As a practical matter, if we have an efficient test design that allows us to accurately predict the effort, the end dates can be established based on calculation rather than hope, and so, the test engineer actually can reduce this second cause.

Deploying too many bugs is a very expensive proposition. The most direct cost is that it costs much, much more to repair a bug after it has been shipped. Indirect costs include harm to the business trying to use the buggy code.

Problem 3: Test Engineers Don't Get Requirements

How could it be that the requirements are missing or incomplete? Let's focus on the typical IT shop, where much of the work of the software folks is to update or modify existing or legacy products. Many of these are quite old, and no one can find the requirements, if they ever existed in the first place. This is all too common, but even more likely is that the legacy application has undergone many modifications over time, and folks thought that they did not need to update the original documentation. Wrong answer, but there you are.

The resulting costs for this problem are high. From the test engineers' point of view, deciding what to test is very difficult. From a developers' point of view, maintaining the application is much harder than it should be. From the users' point of view, no one is really sure what the application is supposed to be doing. Life is tough all around.

Three Problems, One Solution

Maybe life isn't so tough all around. There is a simple, straight-forward technique that will solve all three of these problems. It is called **Behavioral Modeling**, and most of this book is devoted to showing precisely how to go about it. As you will see, Behavioral Modeling directly addresses the first two problems, which deal with both test efficiency and test effectiveness. After some discussion of the technique, we will see how Behavioral Modeling is an important part of the solution to the third problem, the lack of complete, correct requirements.

Before we embark on that journey, let's do a little bit of background about testing in general, just to set the tone and make sure we are all on the same page or singing from the same hymnal or whatever cliché you want that means we share a common understanding.

⌘   ⌘   ⌘

We often forget that testing is an engineering discipline, so let's think about what that means. All engineering in general talks about understanding the problem and creating a solution that is efficient and effective.

Without good test design, we sometimes think about testing everything for any application, no matter how trivial. "Everything" can be huge. In fact, it's infinite for most situations. Therefore, we do not test for everything. What we do is to develop a test suite that will do the job. What we are looking for is "good enough." In many ways, this is the essence of engineering: to find a solution that is adequate.

But we must consider other aspects of engineering as well:

- We must have some notion or understanding of the problem.

- We must codify our solution.

- We must show how our solution actually does solve the problem.

This list should sound familiar. These are exactly the same things you do in software engineering to produce the software in the first place. Many things we do as a part of test design very easily translate into use by developers for producing the software!

In fact, I've had situations where the developers, on seeing my test design, wanted to use it to improve their own software design, and so we began sharing these things back and forth. I have introduced test design methodology in a number of client locations. In several places, they actually use the test design methodology as the software design process.

This is important because, as I said before, we do not want to test everything. That could take literally forever. We want to test just enough. There is always a question of how much is enough. And the answer is not terribly simple. The answer is "it depends." In fact, "it depends" is the answer for most of the questions in this business, but let's talk about what it depends on in this particular case. It depends on **risk.** For low-risk applications, you don't need to test so deeply. If it's a high-risk application or system, you must test more.

So now we need to discuss what risk means. Risk really is a combination of two things:

- The cost of failure

- The likelihood of a fault or a mistake

We measure the cost of failure in both monetary and non-monetary units; the latter is often hardest to measure. In the telecom world, for example, if the system is down, you can calculate the cost in terms of millions of dollars per minute. In the chip world, you can calculate the cost for replacing the microchip when a defect is discovered in the field, but this cost does not necessarily include damage done to the producer's reputation. Some defects can cause disastrous results. One example is the control system in an airplane. Anything on which human life depends could have a very high cost of failure and is, therefore, high risk.

The other factor to consider is the likelihood of failure. A number of factors influence this. Let's list just a few:

- *The understanding of the requirements.* Requirements are generally the statement of the problem. If these are wrong, incomplete, or unclear, the odds go up that the software will be solving the wrong problem.

- *The inherent complexity of the problem.* Face it—some things are just hard! If you are trying to solve a complex problem, then the odds go up that a mistake will be made in the solution.

- *The skill of the development team.* This really has several components:

  o Familiarity with the problem domain.

  o Familiarity with the programming language and approach.

  o Familiarity with the application and production platforms.

For measuring the likelihood of failure, it is sufficient to use just two or three values for each. Consider high/low or high/medium/low. When figuring out the risks associated with the software, you need to merge the two components, cost and likelihood.

The basic notion is that we design our test suite in great depth for the high-risk areas, and we lighten up a bit on the low-risk ones. How much to lighten up is as much a philosophical question as a technical one. The point is that you don't want to spend any more time, money, or effort than you need to. Understanding the risks involved helps us determine how much we "need to."

Another reason for this risk analysis is that it allows us to prioritize the testing effort. One of the harsh realities is that testers rarely have all the time they want. This means you had better organize the testing so that you do the important stuff first. "Important" means to make sure the customers get the most out of the product. Focus on the highest risk areas and expand from there as time and resources permit.

We are unlikely to be able to remove all of the defects in anything we test. Therefore, it behooves us to remove all the defects that would have disastrous results. If something has a high probability of going wrong, then you better make sure that the most probable errors will be detected during the testing, not after the product has been deployed. You want to reduce the number of defects and the number of failures seen by the users.

The basic thing to realize is that **every decision you make in testing is a risk decision.** (Well, every decision you make in life is a risk decision, but let's just stay focused on testing, shall we?)

TESTING

As we look around, we see the word "test" used in a variety of ways. For example, people take a car for a test drive; teachers give tests in school; mechanical engineers test materials to destruction; teenagers test their parents' limits. (Maybe this last is a variant of test-to-destruction!) And, of course, software engineers test their code. Let's look a little closer at this last one. After all, that's where we focus our attention.

So what does it mean to test software? Well, at its most basic level, testing means running the thing you are testing.[1] What this means is the thing must already exist; we are not talking about proving concepts based on software engineering or prototypes or algorithmic analysis or any of those things. For testing, we take the real thing and run it. Testing is "running the thing."

One of the elements to worry about here is: **what** exactly is the thing we are running? Is it entirely complete, or do we have just a portion of the product? Is it some hot-off-the-keyboard version just cobbled together by someone on the project? If so, how do we know just what changes have been made? How do we know what features have been added or what bugs have been fixed since the last time we ran it? And, if some disastrous problem shows up, how do we get back to the previous version to restart the process?

As we think about these questions, it becomes obvious that the thing we are testing needs to be controlled. The software should be under some form of control process. We usually call this process *Software Configuration Management* or SCM.[2] Some very good SCM tools are available on the market. Investing in them will save you.[3]

Another element to worry about is **where** you are going to run the thing. To be really efficient, testing should be in parallel with development. The version the developers are working on will lead the test version by some amount and is apt to be quite volatile (and unstable), so the testing cannot be in exactly the

---

1 The "thing you are testing" is often called either System Under Test (SUT) or Article Under Test (AUT) in the literature.

2 Some people call this *code control*. I don't care what you call it, just be sure you do it!

3 Notice I didn't say save you money or time or effort!

same environment. This means that test planning must consider the test environment and infrastructure.

The third element to consider is **how** you are going to run the thing. Will you use test automation? If not, why not? Keep in mind that you had better have a very good reason to test manually, because, in general, it is not a good idea. We will talk more about test automation later.

To recap, we defined testing as running the thing, but just running the thing is not enough. After you run it, something happens. Is that something right or wrong? Was what happened supposed to happen? Whenever we test something, we should have an idea of what is supposed to occur. This might be, "Claude Monet's loan has been approved," or, "Execution continues to completion with a graceful exit." It is probably not, "We get a blue screen." The point is that testing is more than just running the thing. Testing is **running the thing looking for specific outcomes**.

When you create a test case, you specify not only what the tester is to do but also what constitutes success. You set up pass/fail criteria for your test. It makes sense to document the criteria rather than relying on the memory and knowledge of anybody who might run the test. And after the tests are documented, they should be kept under configuration management. Ideally, they should be stored in the same control system you use for the software.

After you define the pass/fail criteria, you can then know if your product is working correctly or not. Another nice thing about establishing pass/fail criteria is that it becomes possible to turn over the execution of tests to an automated testing tool. This tool can be trained to look for those outcomes for you. It turns out that there is an even more powerful reason to predict the outcomes, which we will discuss later in the test design chapter.

Recapping yet again, we have defined testing as "running the thing looking for specific outcomes." But even this is not enough.

"Running the thing" can be pretty random. You have no real knowledge of how much of the product has been even looked at, let alone exhaustively tested. You need to direct your activities to get broad coverage of the product. This means that a thorough analysis of the functionality and the architecture is required so that you can create a test suite that covers the product in the minimum number of test cases. Why minimum?

- So that we can get the product into users' hands as quickly as possible.

- So that we can cut down time-to-market to the level where we can deliver a product confidently in the least amount of time.

To make sure that we have fully covered all the aspects of the product, we need to control the inputs and environments of the tests as much as possible. This allows us to specify how to run the thing, how to respond to the questions it asks, how to prime the database, and a host of other elements.

There are several very good reasons for doing this:

- One has already been already covered: So that we have maximum coverage with minimum effort.

- Another is this: The better we specify the inputs and environments, the more likely we can automate the entire job of testing. It is, after all, pretty hard to tell a test tool to "bang away" at the article under test.

- And another: Suppose you ran the thing and got some funny result. In most shops, you, the test engineer, then discuss this with the software engineer.

  "Something funny happened," you say.

  "What were you doing?" he or she asks. Note that this is not only a reasonable question, it is often the only way to solve the problem.

  "Well, um..." is **not** a good answer!

- Yet another: You get a fix to the problem. You now must recreate the exact situation you had before in order to confirm that the problem has, indeed, been fixed.

So now we have reached the full, entire definition of software testing. Testing means

- running the thing:

- under known conditions

- looking for specific outcomes

In many organizations, people take the need to test software for granted. They never really examine why they do it. Isn't it interesting that companies spend literally millions of dollars on a task without clear goals? If we better understand why we are doing a task, we have a much better chance of getting out of it what we need. Or, to put it another way, if you don't know where you're going, you probably won't get there.

Let's ask ourselves this question: why do we test software programs? I've asked this question in many settings in many organizations. Most folks look a bit blank for a while and then come up with an answer. The answer usually comes back: we test to show the program works.

Is this really true? (Here's a hint—if I thought it was true, I wouldn't bother to ask!)

I'll tell you what; let's assume that it **is** true, that we do test to show that a program works. Let's take that assumption and see where it leads us.

To begin with, we need to take a closer look at testing itself. There are two basic styles of testing—*black box* and *white box*. Most people use a combination of these styles, but we will consider them separately to make the explanation easier.

Black Box Testing

Let's start with black box testing. In black box testing, all we know about the software is its externals. We can know the inputs and the expected outputs, but we have no knowledge whatsoever about how the program is coded. The internal design is a black box. This style of testing relies on an understanding of the requirements and functional specifications of the software. That's why it is sometimes known as *specification-based testing.*

"Oops. Functional specs; there's a problem," you say. "The stuff I'm working on doesn't **have** functional specs."

Common mistake! All software has functional specifications; they are just not always written down! "We all understand what's needed. Let's just do it."

Another common mistake—and far worse!—is when specs are "understood." Different people have different "understandings." If you write them down, review them, and discuss them, you can avoid a whole raft of problems.

So, if you have decided to use a black box approach to testing, your first task is to study the specification. Sometimes this means interviewing the developers. You need to understand what is expected for all conditions. (Remember our basic definition: testing means running the thing under known conditions, looking for specific outcomes.)

"But wait," you say. "You can't always know everything that's going on in the system."

True, there are times when this is the case, but for most applications, that's a "so what?" You can control enough to do the job. Sometimes this means running in an isolated environment; sometimes this means simulated environments or conditions. It's a bit like the difference between the mathematician and the engineer. Where the mathematician may throw up his or her hands at some impossible condition, the engineer says, "I can get close enough to do some good."

Let's take a trivial example: a little function we will call *bigger*. The function takes two numeric values as input. It returns a value "+1" if the first of the two inputs is bigger than the second, hence the very clever name of the function. It returns a value of "-1" if the first number is smaller than the second, and, finally, it returns a value of "0" if the numbers are equal.

That's it. That is the entire, complete specification of *bigger*. See, I told you it was trivial. (You might want to remember this little function; we will be coming back to it later.)

Okay, now test to show that *bigger* works. Let's see. We know nothing about the internals; so, in order to be sure that *bigger* will give us the correct answer for all valid number pairs, we need to enter all valid number pairs to make sure we get the correct answer.

This, you may quickly realize, is a **very** big number of tests[4]. This means that testing this trivial function will take a **very** long time.

But wait! This is only part of the job. What I've just described only checks out the valid inputs. We are trying to show that the program works. Well, works means two things: the program does what it's supposed to do and does **not** do what it's **not** supposed to do.

Whatever we are testing must be robust enough to correctly diagnose invalid conditions and react accordingly to them. "React accordingly" may mean issue an error message, ask the user for clarification, or any number of other possible responses. Note that the complete entire specification for *bigger* doesn't address this question.

Folks, we have just uncovered a defect in the specification! This is even more important than discovering defects in code, and we did it just by thinking about test design. Why is this more important? Studies have shown that somewhere around 70–80 percent or more of the defects are introduced in the design stage, not the code. If

---

4 Some of you may be thinking that this is an infinite number, and in the abstract, you are correct. But keep in mind that we are talking about a piece of software that runs on a finite machine, so there really is a limit. But it's big.

we can identity and fix the early defects, then the product is better with a lot less effort.[5]

For *bigger*, we will make the assumption that invalid inputs will be detected and handled. Therefore, we need to check out invalid inputs. This could mean entering things that aren't numbers or entering an incorrect number of parameters.

So now how long will it take to test *bigger*? A very, very long time! But we all know that testing should not be so long that the product is obsolete by the time you finish testing it. This shows us that even with something as trivial as *bigger*, trying to show the program works through black box testing is not really possible.

Okay, if black box testing doesn't solve the problem, let's try white box testing. Let's see if white box testing will get us to the goal of showing that the program works.

White Box Testing

In white box testing, we know all there is to know about the programs, including each and every line of code. In fact, white box testing usually works best if the tester is the person who wrote those lines of code. The objective is to develop a set of test cases or a test suite that, when executed, completely covers the product.

"Okay, that's good," you nod. "But what does 'cover' mean?" I'm glad you asked.

---

5 I once knew a man who had an interesting thought. He said that since most of the defects are introduced during design, let's just skip that part and not introduce the bugs. I HOPE he was just kidding.

There are several levels of coverage to consider. At its most basic, we have *statement coverage.* This means that the test suite has executed every statement of the program you are testing at least once. But statements often are composed of component parts, or segments, so we may want to consider *segment coverage,* which means that the test suite has executed every segment of every statement of the program you are testing at least once. Some good tools are available that measure statement coverage and segment coverage, and they should be used.

So now you have to ask if this is enough. I mean, so what if you can execute all the segments? Is this really all that is necessary? No. It is also important to understand the order in which you do things.

So we must also consider *path coverage.* In path coverage, we ask if every possible flow through the logic of the software has been exercised.

Keep this in mind: for any but the most trivial programs, the number of paths can be enormous. In some situations, it may even be considered infinite! So, instead of path coverage, we look at *decision coverage* or *condition coverage.* Decision coverage, also called *branch coverage*, looks at the outcome of comparisons. The logic follows either the TRUE branch or the FALSE branch, for example.

Condition coverage looks at the inputs to the comparisons. Consider the following:

$$\text{If } (A + B) \dots$$

In this expression, A and B are the *conditions.* Condition coverage dictates that we examine cases for **A** true or false and **B** true or false, without regard to the branch taken as a result of this.

Again, we are really looking to cover all the logic paths through the article under test, but usually we cannot do this. On the other hand, we know all we need to know about the program, so maybe we can sort of wave our hands and fudge around a little bit and sort of claim to have fully tested the paths of the program. (Not really, but play along with me here.)

Let's assume you could fully white box test something. Even if you could (which you can't), what would you have shown? Simply this: the program does what the program does. Or in other words, you have shown that the program does what the programmer thought it was supposed to do. Is this really what you want? (Well, if you're the programmer, sure. But the rest of us might be a bit skeptical.) Remember, **a program can be correct without being the correct program!**

What does this leave us with? We are trying to show that the program works, and we have only black box or white box testing at our disposal. Black box testing, as we showed earlier, can never be complete. White box testing can never be sufficient.

To sum it all up, if you set out to show a program works through testing, **you cannot do it**!

If you think about it for a minute, you will realize that testing cannot really show that a program works; it can only show what doesn't work. So now let's adopt an old marketing adage (with apologies to old marketers): *if you can't fix it, feature it!*

Since testing can only show what doesn't work, we should use that as our purpose.

Why Test?

We test in order to find bugs. The whole point is to scrub the product clean before it ships.

"How clean," you ask?

"Clean enough for the customers."

Of course this brings up the notion of test exit criteria, but that's another story.

Let's examine the purpose a little closer. There are several things to infer from this.

Find isn't Fix

Testing isn't debugging. It's identifying the defects so that you can decide what to do about them. This may sound like heresy, but it is not necessary to fix all the bugs. It is, however, necessary to know about them so you can **decide** whether to fix them or not.

Test Choices

Because we are trying to find the bugs and testing can be infinite, we should wisely choose to spend most of our time in areas where the bugs are either likely to exist or where Real Bad Things would happen if bugs were there. Another thought, if you set out to find bugs, you have a better chance of finding them than if you set out to show the program works.

Separate Responsibility

If you are trying to find bugs, you will do better if you are not the person who wrote the code. The person who wrote the code may have made some error in design, and that same error could be reflected in the test.

Besides that, keep in mind that test engineering is a separate discipline from software engineering. It is a good thing if we have separate responsibilities for developing the product and developing the test. (Notice that I said "developing the test" not "testing." The question of who executes the test is not very important. In fact, my vote is for automated test execution, but that is the subject of another day.)

So, while all this may be interesting, it does not really get to heart of the question, "Why do we need to design the test suite?"

Think back to the definition of *bigger*. As we saw, it is possible to test forever. This is **not** a good thing. And remember, just by the process of designing test cases, we are able to detect defects in the specification. This **is** a good thing.

We need to test "just enough." Test design will allow us to determine how much this is.

STAGES OF TESTING

People often speak of tests as though it is all one thing. The truth is, there are many different types of tests, all with their own purposes and practices. In this section, I shall attempt to describe some of the more common types and give a brief description of them.
There is no particular order to this, so just take them as they come. And keep in mind that different organizations may use different terms to mean the same thing.

Development Test

You sometimes hear the phrase "development test." When you hear this, it may mean one of two things. Most commonly, it refers to the testing done by the developer of the software. Rarely is it a separate phase of the process. Developers tend to code a little, try a little, code a little more, and so on. A development test is, by its very nature, a white box activity, that concentrates on path coverage over small regions.

Sometimes, the phrase "development test" is used to distinguish organizational responsibility. Some companies have a separate test department, which maintains an arms-length attitude toward the developers and the product. Some development departments want a greater sense of confidence that their product will pass the scrutiny of the independent testers, so they establish a test department within their own area.

Regression Test

One of the unfortunate facts of software life is that code depends on other code. What precedes a section of code has implications (sometimes adverse). This means that any time one changes **anything** in software, there is the possibility of an unwanted side effect.

Any time one changes anything in software, something that used to work may stop working. When that happens, we say the product has "regressed." Regression testing is about the re-execution of your test suite to make sure that previously successful test cases still run correctly.

This is the area where test automation really pays off. Since the objective is to rerun test cases that have already been run, it makes good sense to have saved them, and even more sense to be able to re-create exactly what you did before, without any manual effort at all. Test tools are especially useful here.

Of course, there are some implications to be aware of. In order to automate regression testing successfully, the organization needs a good process and infrastructure. Automated regression testing also requires a stable test suite. If tests keep changing, you will have a hard time determining where any differences show up.

Another thing needed is an in-depth test design so that you can be sure that the test suite fully covers the product. Otherwise, defects may have been introduced by the changes to the software that you will be unable to detect.

Finally, you need to have records of previous runs to point out where the differences occur.

Prototype Testing

You sometimes hear about a type of testing called prototype testing. This is useful in environments where prototyping is used as a design tool. One creates a prototype and tests certain aspects of the product. For example, you can test the usability or, with modeling techniques, the expected performance.

I remember one company where the development staff used prototyping to design their mainframe application. The VP of engineering, in a brilliant move, decreed that the prototype **had** to be on a PC! Why was this brilliant? Because he knew, without a doubt, if the sales force saw a working model, they would pressure the developers to release the prototype rather than waiting for the real thing.

Performance Testing

Performance testing is actually a bit of an anomaly. Remember our basic purpose for testing is to find defects. With performance testing, rather than looking for defects, *per se*, we are looking for ways to improve the performance of the item under test. The improvements may be in throughput, transaction rate, processing volumes, or any other measure that is important to the success of this particular item.

Rather than the traditional pass/fail measures, performance testing results in numbers to be analyzed. In addition to raw numbers, you may also determine where bottlenecks occur.

A common outcome of performance testing is that areas of the article under test are rewritten or even redesigned to effect an improvement. Another common occurrence is that performance targets are sometimes modified to match the results!

Function Testing

Function testing is the heart of the testing effort. This is where an independent view is taken of the article under test to validate that it functions as specified. For many projects, this phase takes the most time and identifies most of the defects. That is why we need to focus our attention on this phase to be sure that we are doing enough, and just enough, testing.

System Testing

To understand what system testing is all about, we must first understand the distinction between requirements and specifications. This distinction can be quite subtle, but the easiest way to state it is this: requirements identify the problem, while specifications deal with a solution to the problem. Notice that says "**a** solution," not "**the** solution." In identifying the problem, requirements should take on all viewpoints, not just that of the end user. The shorthand way of listing all the factors to be considered goes under the name of the "–ilities."

- Adaptability

- Functionality

- Maintainability

- Portability

- Reliability

- Supportability

- Usability

And the non-"ility" ilities:

- Completeness

- Consistency

- Correctness

- Performance

Let me go sideways for a little bit to give an example. One of the problems we have in modern society is traffic.[6] Our requirement is to solve the traffic problem. The solutions could include more roads, wider roads, more mass transit, more carpools,

---

6 One friend once told me that people in the Bay Area spend three hours a day on traffic—two hours commuting and one hour talking about it with their colleagues.

teleportation, or recession. We will take building more roads as our solution. The specification, then, would talk about things like the number of lanes, the width of the lanes, the depth of the paving material, and a variety of other things all related to the new roads.

Function testing would verify that the specifications have been met. Do the roads conform?

System testing, on the other hand, asks a different question—has the problem been solved? Have the requirements been met? During a system test, we ask, "Has the traffic improved?"

Test Design: Behavioral Modeling

So far we've talked about the value of testing and the stages of testing. But that is not the reason you're reading this book. I suspect you already have at least a pretty good handle on what that's about. I felt it was necessary to have this stuff in the book just for folks who aren't quite as experienced.

But now it's time to get down to it. Let's think about how we design our test. For most organizations, the test design process can be described as "smart folks dream up cool things to do." There is a better way, and that is what this book is about.

That better way is to go through a process that we could think of as modeling the behavior of the article under test. How do we go about making this model? We do this graphically. Any tool will do, I suspect; although, I'll tell you that the one that I use most successfully is Visio®. Many of you have experience with this one; if you do, I recommend using it. I'm not trying to sell you any one graphic application over another. This just happens to be the one with which I'm most familiar.[7]

---

7 In the coming pages, basic shapes will be used to convey concepts that will be explained as they are introduced. The shapes can be found in **Appendix A – Behavioral Model** Glossary. With Visio®, you can buid a stencil based on these shapes.

With Behavioral Modeling, what we do is take a look at the functionality of the article under test at a very high level. Then we begin to lay out, in very broad terms, the process flow from the external user's point of view. In some ways, creating these graphics is a bit like riding a bicycle. You can't really learn how to ride bicycles by reading a book. You have to get out there and start pedaling away. And so, in order to pedal away, you will see a sample.

Bigger

We're going to start with a very simple example. Earlier we discussed a little thing called *bigger*. *Bigger* is a very trivial example. We know that; we said that before. Let's take a look at what a picture would look like for modeling the behavior of *bigger*.

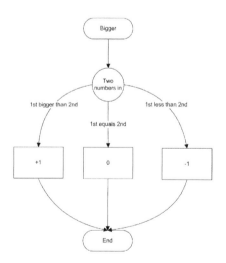

Figure 1: *Bigger* **behavioral model (1)**

First, let's examine the shape of the blocks used in this model. First, we see the oval:

Figure 2: Terminator

This symbol marks the beginning or end of the model.

Next is the circle:

Figure 3: Case

The circle represents case logic. It indicates that any of several possibilities may be chosen.

Third is the rectangle:

Figure 4: Result

The rectangle indicates the expected result of executing a test along the indicated path. You should know that including the result in the behavior model is not strictly necessary. It is here for clarification; but, in some situations, putting the result symbol in the model actually makes it more complex, thus harder to use. In these situations, it is perfectly valid to leave it out.

As we look at *bigger*, we clearly see three branches. Each branch represents a separate test case. This graphic shows us each test case and the expected results from that test case.

This example is, as I said, quite trivial, but it is not too soon to begin asking ourselves exactly how we know what the behavioral model looked like. The basic questions we ask ourselves are

- "What does it do?" and,
- "What influences the behavior?"

What does it do? It is a piece of software that reads in two numbers and compares them. It reports the relationship between them.

What influences the behavior? The relative values of the numbers.

Notice that something subtle is happening here. That first circle says "two numbers in." What if they aren't numbers? What if there are more than two of them? Fewer than two? Our specification for *bigger* missed these important points. When we lay things out graphically, it becomes much clearer. This helps us to identify things that are missing or unsaid or assumed. Let's redraw the model considering a few more points.

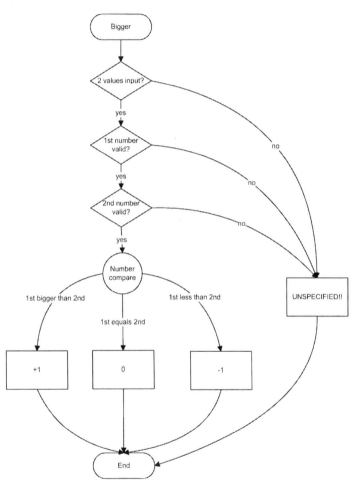

Figure 5: *Bigger* **behavioral model (2)**

We have introduced a new shape in the model: the diamond.

Figure 6: Decision

The decision block represents a binary choice: yes or no; true or false. If you are familiar with flowcharts, you will recognize this symbol, but there is an important distinction between a flowchart and a behavioral model. In a flowchart, the logic of the program is described. At a decision point, the program asks a question and reacts to the answer. In a behavioral model, there is no question. The decision block represents the choices the test designer makes. Thus, we do not ask if there are, for example, two input values. We will set up tests such that on one path there will be two values and on the other there will not be. So, as a style point, we do not use question marks in the text for a decision block.

When we look at this diagram, we can see the very powerful reason for predicting the results of any one particular test. Notice those three paths that go to the box labeled "UNSPECIFIED." What we have done is identify defects in the specification merely by attempting to diagram the functionality. When we remember that 70–80 percent of the defects in software are introduced at the requirements or specification phase, we can see that the mere act of diagramming the function as we've done here helps us to improve the product.

So, we have identified a hole in the specification. What does the developer do faced with a hole in the specification? That depends on the developer's level of experience. The very experienced senior developer, faced with a hole, will go back to whoever produced the specification, ask what is supposed to happen, and make sure that the specification is updated with this information. The intermediate developer will try to "figure out" what's supposed to happen and code to that. What does the rookie do? Nothing. The rookie won't even notice that there is a hole in the specification.

And what about the tester? The same thing. Our tests must conclude whether or not the program works as specified. But before that, we must be sure the specification is complete, clear, and correct. Notice that in the diagram above, we left the results as "unspecified." In some situations, the tester needs to sort of figure out what's going on. We need to keep those to a minimum. The way to figure out what is going on is to go back to the author of the specification, get clarification, and **make sure the specification is updated with the clarification**. That's the only way to be sure that the entire team has the same understanding.

Testers should never make up specifications. If you find yourself doing this, stop it! Stop it right now!

Our task is to find the defects, remember? The real problem is that when we make up a specification, the developer may also be making up a specification. The specification that the tester makes up and the specification that the developer makes up may differ, and then we wind up with a mismatch between the testing and the developing.

One question that often comes up is this: what is the best way to reduce the number of problems in requirement and specification documents? The answer is actually quite simple. The single most important thing you can do for your software is to conduct formal reviews, or verifications. What we are talking about in this book really is a safety net in case some things slip through. We do not address verification in detail in this book. Many fine books, papers, and articles are available on the subject, and I recommend you check them out. For those of you with some curiosity, however, we will have an overview of verification in **Appendix D** – Verification.

Back to *bigger*. We have more things to consider. For example, we could think about the type of data we have. We have numbers. Are they decimal? Are they scientific notation? But I think for our purposes, we've gotten enough information from here. The whole point is to show you the graphics. We are going to show a more complex example very soon. For now, go back, look at what we've done, and think about it. I'll wait here.

⌘   ⌘   ⌘

Welcome back.

While it may be hard to see with something as simple as *bigger*, keep in mind that there is not necessarily a one-to-one correspondence between paths in the behavioral model and number of test cases. It is close, but, in some situations, there may be either more or fewer test cases than paths.

Let's look at an example to illustrate this point. Suppose that *bigger* could execute on any of three different platforms: Windows, Mac, and Unix. If this were the case, the behavioral model would need to account for this. The resulting model would look like this:

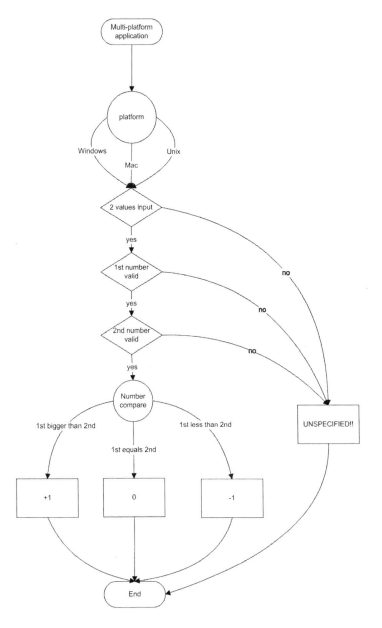

Figure 7: *Bigger* **behavioral model (3)**

If you count the number of paths through the model, you find a total of eighteen paths—the six we started with, multiplied by the number of platforms. If the architecture is such that the same executable code is used in each of the platforms, then you could plan the test cases so that some of them are executed in one platform, some others in another platform, and the remainder in the final platform, thus dropping from eighteen test cases back to the original six. The decision is, as usual, a risk decision.

Finally, let's clean up the "UNSPECIFIED" result. We will have gone back to the author of the specification, reported this problem, and the specs will have been updated. We now know that the return codes are as follows:

Condition	Return Code
FIrst number bigger than second	+1
First number equal to the second	0
First number smaller than the second	-1
Not two imput values	-97
First input value non-numeric	-98
Second input value non-numeric	-99

Table 1 Bigger return codes

Finally, we have the real, complete behavior model for *bigger:*

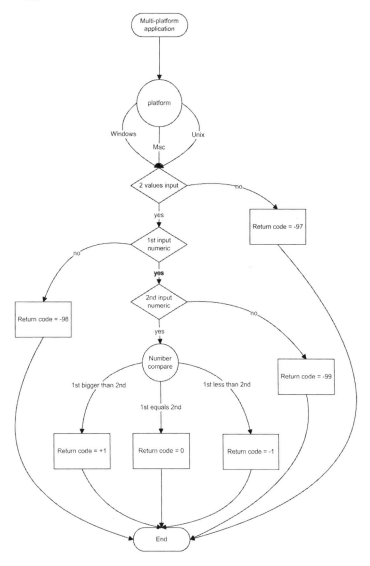

Figure 8: Final *bigger* **behavioral model**

Also, please keep reminding yourself that this is **not** a flowchart. It is a behavioral model of the test design. An example demonstrates this quite clearly a bit later on.

FAST

Let's try something a bit more complex than *bigger*. In this next example, we introduce a few more concepts.

Let's consider a banking application. In this case, it's the familiar automated teller machine or ATM. Our ATM is a very, very simple one. It can't do very much. But that's okay. We don't need it to do very much. We just need it to show us how to do test design.

We call our ATM the Functionally Advanced Sidewalk Teller, or *FAST*. Okay, I admit it; *FAST* is not terribly functionally advanced. All it can do is deposit to or withdraw from either a checking account or a savings account, transfer money between those two accounts, or tell you your balance in either of the accounts.

Even though it's a pretty simple application, to try and diagram all of it on one page would be difficult. What we're going to do is to divide it into subsections. We call this process *functional decomposition*. With functional decomposition, we divide the article under test into independent areas. When I say independent, I really am talking about an operational definition of the term. We look for parts of the application that can be tested independently from the other parts. Of course, there's always interaction in a computing product; however, we try and look for ways to minimize this in our test design.

Let's try a first pass at the functional decomposition of *FAST*. What is it? What does it do? Look at this diagram:

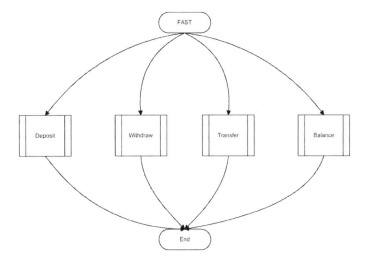

Figure 9: *FAST* **behavioral model (1)**

We have just introduced another shape: the striped rectangle:

Figure 10: Defined process

This is called a *defined process*. This means that the process is defined in a lower-level diagram.

Let's look a bit closer at this example. For *FAST*—as well as every other example one can think of—you, the tester, must supply your own external knowledge to the article under test.

When you walk up to a teller machine, the first thing you do is put in your card—that little piece of plastic the bank gave you—and type in your password. This is sometimes called a PIN, which stands for Personal Identification Number. Some people call this a PIN number, which of course then means personal identification number number, but that's a different subject.

We need to include a defined process examining the sign-in functionality. So let's add this to our diagram for the test suite.

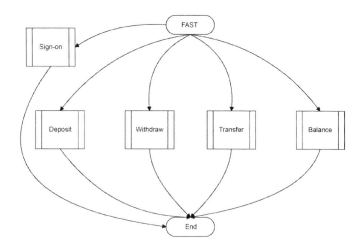

Figure 11: *FAST* **behavioral model (2)**

"But wait," you say. "Don't we have to sign on in order to do anything? Why do we need a separate defined process for signing on?"

Good question. Let's do some arithmetic. Assume for the moment that there are ten different paths through the *sign-on* functionality and ten different paths through *deposit*. If we were to test them both together, then that would mean one hundred different ways to get through the combination of *sign-on* and *deposit*, or one hundred test cases. If we test them separately, there are only twenty test cases. We always look for ways to add the number of test cases, not multiply the numbers.

This suggests some very important principles of functional decomposition.

Using something isn't testing it. We <u>use</u> *sign-on* to get to the other functions, but we only <u>test</u> *sign-on* in its own set of test cases.

Assume the things not being directly tested are perfect. This is a very difficult assumption, I know; but it is a very important one in simplifying our test suite. Assume that *sign-on* "works" and get on with the business of testing *deposit*. To put it another way, in testing *deposit*, we don't really care if all of the ins and outs of *sign-on* are correct, as long as we can find any that allow us to move ahead.

Now we're getting there. Let's think about this again. There's a certain amount of commonality among those various actions one can take. If we look at some of the error cases, or exceptional cases, we can say that, in general, it doesn't matter whether you're trying to deposit, withdraw, transfer, or get the balance. For example, suppose the printer runs out of paper. Let's create a separate process for these exceptional cases.

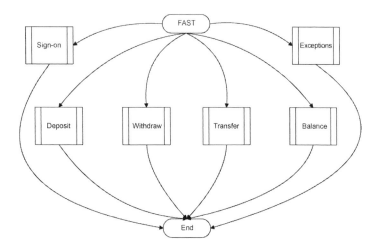

Figure 12: *FAST* behavioral model (3)

That looks kind of like a pumpkin, doesn't it? Some of the groups I've worked with have had a lot of fun with the "looks like" game!

Sometimes, despite our best efforts of decomposing the article under test, we still are left with the possibility of interactions between them. For example, we might wonder if the system under test is left in a precarious state after a function. Just to be on the safe side, we will create one more defined process, one that considers combinations of functions or strings.

The next diagram, then, shows us the complete behavioral model of *FAST*, albeit at a high level.

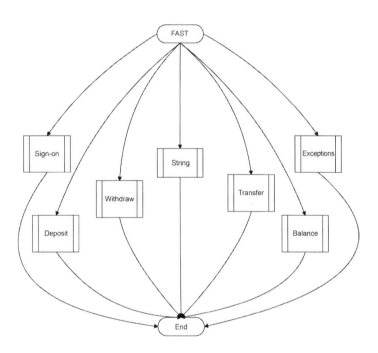

Figure 13: *FAST* behavioral model (4)

This haggis-looking thing is a bit messy, in my opinion. Let's redraw it one more time, a bit more neatly.

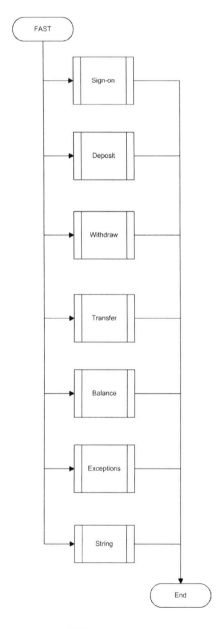

Figure 14 FAST behavioral model (5)

We're going to dive a little deeper and show you some of the test designs for a couple of the lower-level processes. And then we'll see how this stuff all hangs together.

Let's turn our attention to the pre-defined process, *deposit* in this next graphic.

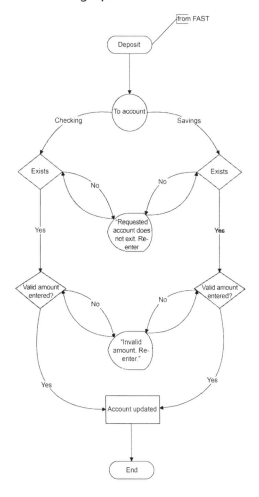

Figure 15: *Deposit* **behavioral model (1)**

Here is a new thing we've introduced. Notice the display symbol:

Figure 16: Display

The display symbol indicates something is displayed on the screen. This is a hint to the tester so that he or she will know what to look for during the test. Within the symbol, we indicate the expected content of the screen. In the examples above, these are the expected error messages. Also notice the lines going into and out of those display blocks. These indicate that in the error condition, an error message displays, and control is returned back to the main line of the processing. Not all programs behave this way. It is actually more common to have a decision point after an error message where the user is asked whether to continue or not.

The display symbol is actually a special case of result. While you may decide not to include result on some paths of your model, it is very rare not to include display.

Let's set the syntax aside and review the example above for content. In the model, if we are on a path where the selected account does not exist, the line indicates that we go back and check again to see if the account exists. What should happen, however, is that we go back earlier in the model—back to selecting the account in the first place. Another thing to notice is that both sides of this diagram are the same; it is symmetrical. This suggests that we can reduce the diagram to something a little bit simpler. Take a look at the following example:

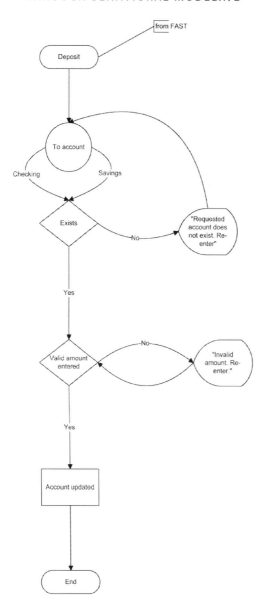

Figure 17: *Deposit* **behavioral model (2)**

You may find a different model of the *deposit* function behavior. In testing, it is very rare to have only one right answer. Let's not spend a lot of time trying to figure out additional alternatives or other solutions. We'll continue to work with this one. This is actually a pretty good analogy to what you do while designing your tests. Come up with a good design: one that works. Don't spend days, weeks, and months agonizing over the one perfect, best, only true answer. There isn't one! Get one that works and move forward.

In these next few diagrams, we highlight the paths for some *deposit* function test cases.

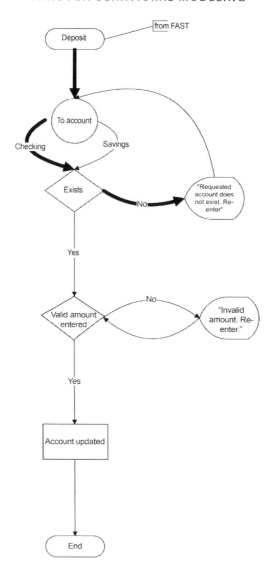

Figure 18: Test path (1)

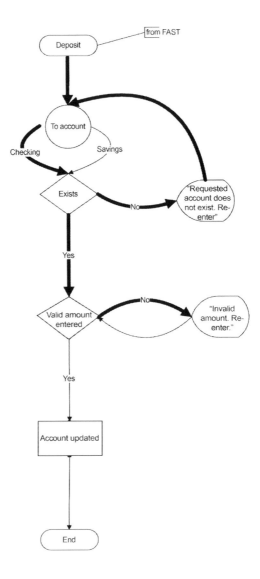

Figure 19: Test path (2)

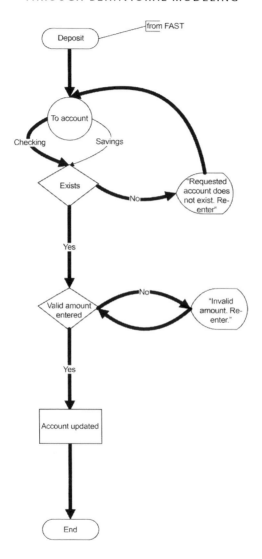

Figure 20: Test path (3)

Okay, I think that's enough of this. You should be able to extend the notion of these test paths yourself by now. It is fairly straightforward. Over the next few pages, I'm going to show you the behavioral model—the test design—for the other functions of *FAST*. Before going on to look at those, I suggest you try these on your own and then compare your answers with mine. If our designs differ, that doesn't mean that yours is wrong or that mine is right. Remember what I said before: There is no one right answer. On the other hand, we will use the design I've come up with in the next section, so you should understand where we differ (if we do) and study these diagrams because we will be using them.

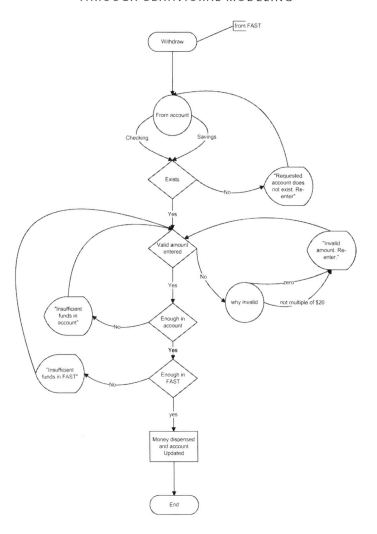

Figure 21: *Withdraw* behavioral model

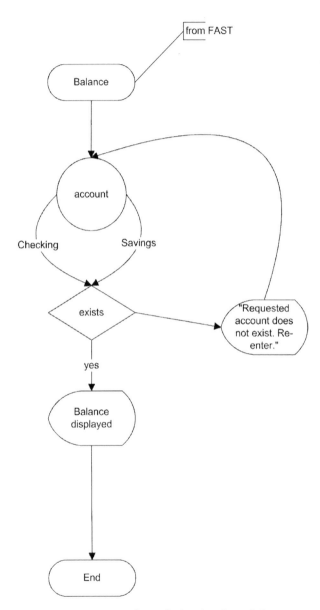

Figure 22: *Balance* **behavioral model**

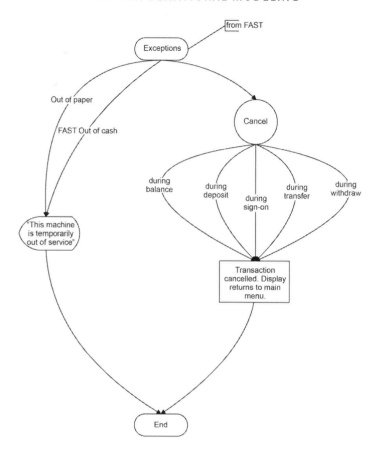

Figure 23: *Exceptions* behavioral model

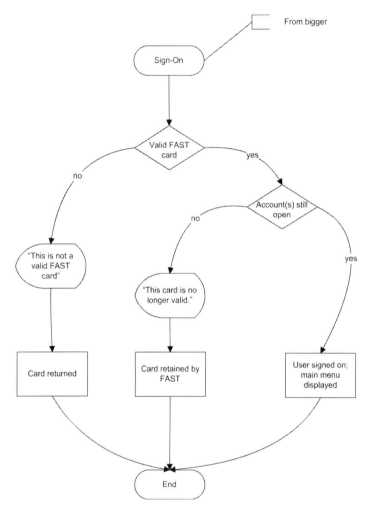

Figure 24: *Sign-on* **behavioral model**

The last function from our high-level behavior model is *string*. In this function, we address the interaction among the other functions. For example, after a withdrawal, is it possible to do a deposit? After a balance, is it possible to do a deposit?

Remember the basic concept of functional decomposition: we assume that the things we are just using are perfect, and we only worry about the specific thing we are testing. For *string*, we are testing the interactions, not the functions that are interacting; so we assume, for example, that deposit is perfect. We will use just a representative sample of the functions we are using. The symbol for a representative sample is the parallelogram:

Figure 25: Representative sample

The behavioral model for *string* looks like this:

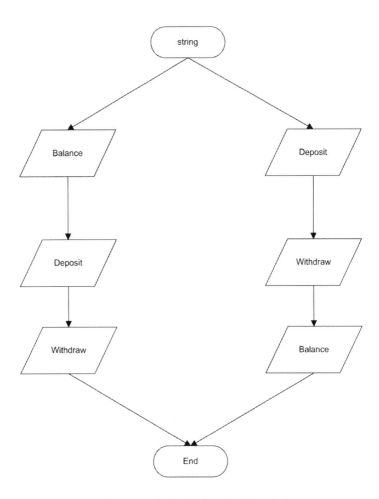

Figure 26: *String* **behavioral model**

This model tells us that we don't much care what subset of *deposit*, *withdraw*, or *balance* test cases are chosen. The details of those functions are tested in other portions of the test suite. Also, I have not indicated that we must try every combination and permutation of the functions as a part of *string*. This is strictly a judgment call. Sometimes you need to do this, and sometimes you may decide whether that would be overkill. The point is to think about it. Do an analysis based on your experience and make the decision that is in the best interests of the project and the users of the article under test. Weigh the benefit of more testing against the delay in delivering the article to the people who need it.

Keep in mind: every decision you make in testing is a risk decision. This includes how much testing you do. Balance the risk of missing a bug against the risk of missing a deadline.

Triangle

Consider this classic example: the *triangle* program.

Triangle reads in three values representing the three sides of a triangle. The program determines whether the sides follow triangle rules to form an equilateral, an isosceles, or a scalene triangle.

An equilateral triangle has all three sides the same. An isosceles triangle has two sides the same. For purposes of this problem, we will say that an isosceles triangle has two and only two sides the same; the third side must be different. A scalene triangle has no sides the same.

One rule of triangles is that the sum of any two sides must be greater than the third side. (This must be true for each of the sides.) After analyzing the values, the program either announces the type of triangle, or, if the inputs do not follow all the rules of "triangle-ness," it announces this fact.

Triangle displays one of four messages:

- Equilateral
- Isosceles
- Scalene
- Improper triangle

How shall we model the behavior? Let's ask the basic questions: What does it do? What influences it?

To begin with, it must distinguish between proper and improper triangles. For the proper triangles, it must determine what type they are. Consider this:

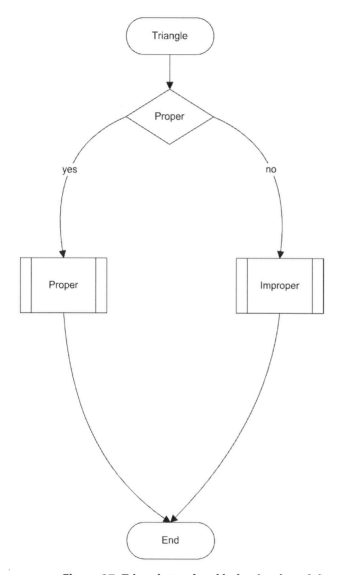

Figure 27: *Triangle* top-level behavioral model

Our test design will look at both proper and improper triangles. This clearly demonstrates what was stated earlier: a behavioral model is **not** a flow chart. It is very unlikely that a software developer would code the triangle program as it appears in the top-level model above.

When we break down the specification in this way, the lower-level models become quite simple.

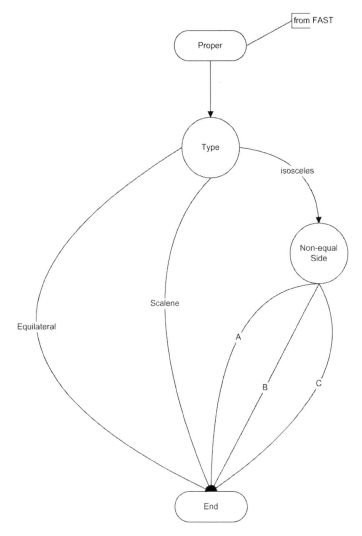

Figure 28: *Proper triangle* behavioral model

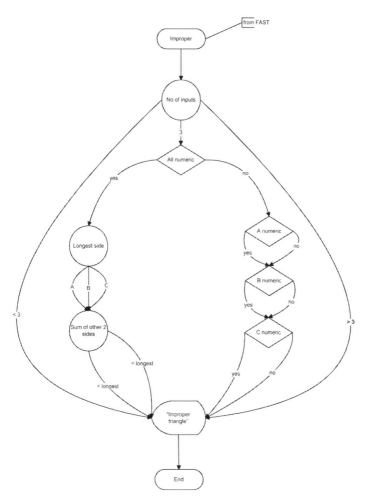

Figure 29: *Improper triangle* **behavioral model**

We did not indicate the lengths of the sides in either of the models above. Nor did we, in the *FAST* example or the *bigger* example, indicate any actual values. There is a reason for this: we don't need to.

For any program, we can envision potentially an infinite number of possible test cases. With our approach, we can describe what a value looks like without worrying about whether the actual length of the side of a triangle is five or six or 167.

We use the concept of *equivalence partitioning*. For any input parameter or field, we can find a set equivalence classes. The members of each set are equivalent to all the other members of the set. If this is so, then one input value is all we need for each set. For example, if we choose a test case for equilateral triangles, all we care about is that the sides are equal. We don't care how long the sides are.

There are, of course, some rules about the values for *triangle*. For example, all the sides must be positive. We assume this, even though the specification did not say so. The specification may have bounded the sides by stating that the sides must be within a specific range. For ranges, there are three equivalence classes. One class is for all values below the range, one class is for all values within the range, and the third class is for all values above the range.

Here is a warning: if you choose to use only one value within a range, it is perfectly valid to do so, and it takes strong nerves! Many of us are used to the notion of doing the same thing over and over in our test cases with slightly different input values. If you truly have identified equivalence classes, then this style of testing is quite wasteful. To switch over can feel a bit uncomfortable at first, but you'll get over it.

Another warning: not all equivalence classes are obvious, and sometimes things that look like they are equivalent really aren't. For example, one person told me about a banking application he was testing where a bug showed up if the customer name had an apostrophe in it. He assured me that the specification did not say anything about this, but you can be sure that this will be one of his test cases from now on!

While we are on the subject of equivalence partitioning, let's talk about a variant that is sometimes useful: *boundary value analysis.* If the input field is a range of values, instead of picking any value within the range, if you are using boundary value analysis, you pick the values at the edges of the range. Since many coding errors occur at these edges, this could be a good way to find them.

Flowerpots

There is another symbol that is often used but did not show up in our examples. It is a manual process and looks like this:

Figure 30: Manual process

The purpose of this symbol is to show the tester where she or he needs to do something. It is a good reminder.

I remember being on a project where I introduced this methodology, and one of the test designs ended in a manual operation at the bottom of the page. The project manager thought that this made the entire diagram look like a flowerpot. From that point on, all test design documents were called flowerpots. "Do you have the flowerpot done for function A?" and, "When is the flowerpot review meeting?"

There was nothing I could do to make them stop! Finally, I gave in and used the same terminology. Even today, I find I am thinking that term and have to correct myself! If I hadn't liked those folks so much, I could be very annoyed with them.

A Few More Thoughts

This is an important rule to follow in constructing these behavior models: the model must fit on one page. If it does not, go back and take a second look at your functional decomposition. It is possible that you need to decompose the article under test a bit further. Never yet have I seen a situation where the article under test could not comply with this rule. Should you see an example, it most likely means that the specification is irreducibly complex. Since defects correlate with complexity, this would indicate that the article under test needs to be redesigned and not just to make life easier for the tester.[8]

On one project I was on, one of the engineers took to heart the admonition that the behavioral model had to fit on one page. The reason for this rule is that this forces us to get down to the simplest component possible. Remember, the driving notion behind functional composition is: find the simple within the complex. Rather than decompose the function as far as it would go, the engineer bent all the lines to make it fit. I have, with that person's permission, reproduced the behavioral model here. Most of the text had been removed, but I think you will get the idea.

---

8 On reviewing this manuscript, I remembered that I have, once and only once, seen this exact situation. The defect rate in that piece of code was the highest in the entire program!

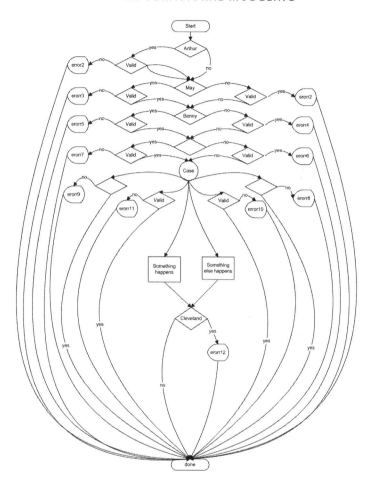

Figure 31: The artichoke

One final note before we leave the topic of test design: As you read this book, it seems a simple task to create a behavior model. You can nod your head as you look at the examples.

Here is a warning and an anti-warning.

Warning: it is harder than it looks. The first time you try this on your own, it will be puzzling and frustrating. You may find yourself swearing under your breath at whoever wrote the functional specifications for the article under test. Those same specs that seemed so clear when you first read them now seem incomplete and ambiguous, and you wonder if they were ever reviewed in the first place.

This is a good thing. By your efforts, you are finding the weaknesses that will sink the project. Be sure to document your findings. [9]

Anti-warning: you were right the first time. It actually is pretty easy to create a behavior model, once you get the hang of it. It just takes a little bit of practice. Most folks struggle with the first one or two, and then it's smooth sailing from then on. Stick with it. Don't be discouraged.

---

9 I recommend using your incident management process to log the errors you have just been cursing. Be sure the process includes indicating where in the process the defect was introduced.

Test Case Design

In the previous section, we talked about test design. Test design is based on a model of the behavior of the article under test. This behavioral model describes the article under test as it will behave when we execute the test suite. The problem now is to design a test suite that implements the test design.

On the development side, developers begin with requirements, move down to specification, and move from there down into logic design. On the testing side, the process is similar. The test design of the previous section serves as the specification for the test suite. We now move to our lower level, which is test case design.

We need to describe the test suite in such a way that we can see the totality of it. If you are simply creating a list of test cases of the form—do this, do that, now do the other thing—this can result in a whole lot of pages that are difficult read, to comprehend, and to grasp as a part of a larger whole.

We are going to lay out test case design on a spreadsheet. There are certain conventions to be used in creating these things. We will discuss these very shortly. The purpose is that the reviewer can see the entire suite at a single glance. Well, maybe a few glances, but you get the idea.

Template

Look at the following template for a test case design:

TCD ID:						
Description:						
Author:						
Original Release:			Date:			
Test Case:						
Control Points:						
Expected Results						

Figure 32: Test case design template

Let's talk about some things we see in this template.

The top section is called the header. It begins with the identifier for the test case design—the TCD. The "TCD ID" is a unique name that helps us to locate it in the hierarchy. We'll talk more about that later.

The "Description" is, as the name implies, a brief description of the function tested in this particular test case design. The name of the author is useful. "Original Release" refers to release of the article under test. As follow-on releases introduce changes to the software, it will be helpful to know which test cases may need to change. The date tells us when this test case design was completed.

The main body of the test case design is divided into two sections. The left-hand column contains the list of control points. A control point is anything that you can control or cause. This control point list is the lowest level of input for the individual test cases.

There is a particular nomenclature for syntax of control points, which we will talk about in just a few minutes as we see some examples. The rest of the main body of the test case design contains a series of columns. Each column represents a test case. Each test case, then, may be thought of as a combination of control points.

The naming of test cases is quite straightforward. You take the name of the test case design and append the number. This is very helpful in complex situations; the test case name can tell you exactly where in the functional mix the test case sits.

The final section of the test case design contains the expected results. Each column represents a test case. At the bottom of each test case we describe what should occur as a result of executing this particular test case.

Let's look at some examples.

Bigger

Our task now is to translate from the behavior model to the test case design.

Step one is to create the list of control points. All you need to do is locate the decision blocks and case blocks in the behavior model. Each choice in the behavior model translates directly into a control point.

Once you have created the control point list, start working with the paths indicated in the behavior model. I like to check them off as I go. Remember, there is not necessarily one test case for every path.

For each column in the test case design, predict the outcome and list it in the "Expected Results" row.

Refer back to Figure 8: Final *bigger* behavioral model on page 50. Our test case design based on this is:

TCD ID:	**B**					
Description:	**Bigger**					
Author:	**Shel Prince**					
Original Release:	**1.0**			Date:	**7/5/20xx**	

Test case:	B01	B02	B03	B04	B05	B06
Control Points:						
Platform:	*	*	*	*	*	*
Windows	*	*	*	*		
Mac					*	
Unix						*
Two values input:	*	*	*	*	*	*
no	*					
yes:		*	*	*	*	*
First value numeric?		N	Y	Y	Y	Y
Second value numeric?			N	Y	Y	Y
First number:				*	*	*
bigger than second				*		
equal to second					*	
less than second						*
Expected Results	retrun code = -97	retrun code = -98	retrun code = -99	retrun code = +1	retrun code = 0	retrun code = -1

Figure 33: Bigger test case design

Let's look at a few of the things we've introduced here. Notice the left-hand column headed "Control Points." In this column you see "Platform." The line ends with a colon. This tells us that the next several lines are subordinate control points under the main control point "Platform." These subordinate control points are indented. In this case the subordinate control points are the three platforms supported by *bigger*. This means that a single test case will have only one of those platforms chosen. There is no limit to the number of levels of subordinate control points. As a general rule, subordinate control points at the lowest level are mutually exclusive.

In the body of the test case design, you will see mostly either blank cells or cells filled with asterisks. The asterisk tells us that something is chosen or exists. For example, notice that "Platform: Unix" is selected in some of the cells or columns but not in others. This tells us that for those test cases where Unix is chosen, we will execute the test case on that platform. The asterisk is merely the existence operator.

Now notice the line that says, "First value numeric?" The question mark tells us that, just as in any other writing, this is a question. It is answered as either Y for yes or N for no.

Another symbol that often appears in test case designs, although not in this example, is the equal sign. For example, had we chosen to specify an actual value for the inputs, we could have put "value =" in the left-hand column and filled in the actual value in the cell for each particular test case. We've chosen not to do that here; rather, we specify the actual value later.

Now, please turn your attention to the last row in the test case design. Here we specify the expected results of the test case execution. Notice several things about this. The formatting, you will notice, is sideways. I realized some time ago that this allows it to be readable and gives you more room for the information you're going to need.

This small example demonstrates some of the power of that technique. Once you are comfortable with this technique, you can simply look at the test case design, notice the pattern, and determine whether you have adequate coverage. Coverage really is one of the primary issues in test design. We always need to know that we sufficiently cover the functionality of the article under test. These test case designs allow us to determine if we have or have not done so.

Well, congratulations! You have completed your first test case design. It may seem a little bit difficult at first; but, keep in mind this is your first attempt. *Bigger* is really quite simple. More complex applications can take longer to analyze. In planning your project, you should consider how long test case design takes. The range, depending on complexity and size of the article under test, could be from a few hours to several weeks. Our one-page rule for behavioral models applies to test case design as well. And, yes, sometimes I use small font.

FAST

So far, we have seen an example of a single-level test case design. These are little to no help for most applications. We use the process of functional decomposition to break up the article under test into manageable units. This is reflected in the behavior models we have already seen. For an example, refer to Figure 14 FAST behavioral model (5) on page 56. How do we show this in a test case design?

Please notice this next template:

TCD ID:		
Description:		
Author:		
Original Release:		Date:

Function:	**TCD:**	**Page:**

Figure 34: High-level test case design template

In this high-level test case design template, we show the hierarchical structure of the article under test. The first column has changed. We no longer think of control points; rather, we think of functions. The next column is headed "TCD" for test case design. Here, we list the identifier for the next level test case design. That next level test case design may be another high-level test case design, or it may be the actual lowest-level test case design.

The third column is for the page number. This may or may not be valuable in your setting. If all of your work is electronic, then you don't need the page number; you simply have hyperlinks from the test case design column to where you want go. On the other hand, in some environments, the test case design is printed, in which case the page number reference proves quite useful for someone trying to find his or her way through the document. Keep in mind that these documents can get fairly involved and very long, so anything that helps the reader is useful.

The high-level test case design for *FAST* looks like this:

TCD ID:	**F**	
Description:	**FAST**	
	Shel	
Author:	**Prince**	
Original Release:	**1.0**	Date: **9/7/20xx**
Function:	**TCD:**	**Page:**
Balance	FB	
Deposit	FD	
Exceptions	FE	
Sign on	FS	
Transfer	FT	
Withdraw	FW	
String	FR	

Figure 35: FAST high-level test case design

Each of the lower-level test case designs is referred to by a name. The name begins with the ID of the current test case design and adds a character that indicates the next level functionality. One advantage of this approach is that once you do the initial functional decomposition, you could assign different pieces of the application to different members of the team.

The good news is this: we now know exactly what the test suite looks like. The bad news? We now must implement the test case design.

Let's look at a couple of the lower-level test case designs. The example below shows the *deposit* function from *FAST*.

Matrix ID:	**FD**					
Description:	**FAST Deposit**					
Author:	**Shel Prince**					
Original Release:	**1.0**		Date:	**9/6/20xx**		
Test case:	FD01	FD02	FD03	**FD04**	**FD05**	**FD06**
Control Points:						
To Account:	*	*	*	*	*	*
Checking	*	*	*			
Savings				*	*	*
Account exists?	N	Y	Y	N	Y	Y
Amount of deposit:		*	*		*	*
valid			*			*
invalid		*			*	
Expected Results	"Requested account does not exist. Re-enter."	"Invalid amount. Re-enter." Re-entered amount accepted.	Account balance updated with the deposited amount.	"Requested Account Does Not Exist. Re-enter."	"Invalid amount. Re-enter."	Account balance updated with the deposited amount.

Figure 36: FAST deposit test case design

One of the control points is called "To Account." The subordinate control points are checking and savings accounts. Now notice the line, "Account exists?" As before, the question mark tells us that this is a question to be answered as either Y or N. Another way to say exactly the same thing is this:

Account Exists:
Yes
No

With this form, asterisks in the appropriate cells give the reader the information needed. You will see an example of this a bit later.

Why would you use one format over the other? The answer depends on what you are trying to communicate to the reader of the test case design. Using the second form above often shows more emphasis on the choice to be made. [10]

Now, let's look at the test case design for the *withdraw* function of *FAST*.

---

10 I confess I sometimes use this format to reduce the number of rows in my test case design so that I can conform to the one-page rule.

Matrix ID: **FW**										
Description:	**FAST Withdraw**									
Author: **Shel Prince**										
Original Release: **1.0**			Date: **9/6/20xx**							

Test case:	FW01	FW02	FW03	FW04	FW05	FW06	FW07	FW08	FW09	FW10
Control Points:										
From Account:	*	*	*	*	*	*	*	*	*	*
Checking	*		*	*	*	*				
Savings		*					*	*	*	*
From Account exists?	N	N	Y	Y	Y	Y	Y	Y	Y	Y
Amount of withdrawal:			*	*	*	*	*	*	*	*
zero			*				*			
more than in "from"				*				*		
Multiple of $20?					Y	Y			Y	Y
More than in FAST?					Y	N			Y	N
Expected Results	"From Account Does Not Exist"		"Cannot withdraw zero."	"Insufficient funds in From Account. Re-enter or cancel."	"Not enough cash to service your request. Re-enter or cancel."	Cash dispensed. Amount deducted from account.	"Cannot withdraw zero."	"Insufficient funds in From Account. Re-enter or cancel."	"Not enough cash to service your request. Re-enter or cancel."	Cash dispensed. Amount deducted from account.

Figure 37: FAST withdraw test case design

In the examples so far, each test case ended with a single column describing the expected results. In the *withdraw* example above, we see two adjacent test cases that have exactly the same expected result. When this happens, we combine the expected results cells into one.

This concept can be very interesting. What if you have three adjacent columns that have some results the same in all three, some results the same in two of the three, and some results unique to each individual test case. In this case, the "Expected Results" row would look like this:

	All three the same		
		Just these two	
Expected Results	individual result for this test case	This part is unique.	and so is this

Figure 38: Expected results for complex outcomes

To see how all this plays together, look at

Appendix C – *FAST* Test Case Design, which contains the entire test case design for *FAST*.

Triangle

These next few pages will show the test case design for *triangle*. As a reference, you may wish to review the behavior models on pages 78–81.

TCD ID:	T		
Description:	High order test design for triangle		
Author:	Shel Prince		
Original Release:	1.0	Date:	**6/5/20xx**
Function:	TCD:	**P**age:	
Improper	TI		
Proper	TP		

Figure 39: Triangle test case design

TCD ID: **TI**									
Description:	**Triangle; Improper triangles**								
Author:	**Shel Prince**								
Original Release: **1.0**				Date: **7/5/20xx**					
Test case:	TI 01	TI 02	TI 03	**TI 04**	**TI 05**	**TI 06**	**TI 07**	**TI 08**	**TI 09**
Control Points:									
Number of inputs:	*	*	*	*	*	*	*	*	*
<3	*								
>3		*							
=3			*	*	*	*	*	*	*
All input numeric:			*	*	*	*	*	*	*
yes:			*	*	*				
Longest side=			A	B	C				
Sum of other two sides:			*	*	*				
= longest			*						
< longest				*	*				
no:						*	*	*	*
A numeric?						N	Y	Y	N
B numeric?						N	Y	N	N
C numeric?						N	N	Y	Y
Expected Results	All test cases result in the message "Improper Triangle"								

Figure 40: Improper triangle test case design

TCD ID: **TP**					
Description:	**Triangle; Proper triangles**				
Author:	**Shel Prince**				
Original Release: **1.0**				Date:	**7/5/20xx**

Test case:	TP 01	TP 02	TP 03	TP 04	TP 05
Control Points:					
type of triangle:	*	*	*	*	*
equilateral	*				
scalene		*			
isosceles:			*	*	*
short side=			A	B	C
Expected Results	Equilateral	Scalene	Isosceles		

Figure 41: Proper triangle test case design

The Three Problems Solved

Let's go back and look at the three basic problems of software testing described in the introduction. They are:

- Testing takes too long
- Testing misses too many bugs
- Test engineers don't have product requirements

We have seen how Behavioral Modeling builds a test suite that is the <u>minimum</u> <u>necessary</u> number of test cases. The "necessary" part assures that the test effort will be as effective as possible. The "minimum" part assures that the testing will be as effective as possible. This takes care of the first two problems in our list. What about the third?

The problem of missing or incomplete requirements can be solved using behavioral models. The secret to this is the very simplicity of the models themselves. They are easy to read and understand. We saw some examples of this earlier. The way we solve the problem is this: the test engineer creates a first-draft model based on interviews with the business folks as well as his or her knowledge or expertise in the problem domain.

This first-draft model forms the basis of a conversation with all the stakeholders who can easily understand, review, and comment on the draft. The draft is then updated and the process continues. Once the model is finished, a requirements document can be created from the model. My personal opinion is that the model itself is sufficient, but there may be value in translating it into text—that's a decision for the business to make.

Test Automation

Some, perhaps most, test cases listed in the test case design can be automated. You should make every effort to automate the test cases. However, you should keep the economics of automation in mind.

To automate a test suite is a project, and it should be treated like one. You need to do advance planning and preparation. You must have resources assigned to the automation project and develop a schedule for it. Depending on your choice of automation approach, it can take two, three, four, or more times as long to automate the test cases than it would to simply run them. In addition to this, unless you are careful with your automation architecture, a minor change in the application in a follow-on release could result in a total rewrite of your entire automated suite.

Most people, unfortunately, do not keep these things in mind. That is why most automation projects fail.

But now, having done the test design and test case design, you have an advantage. Your advantage is that you now know precisely what the test suite should look like. This gives you the opportunity to select those test cases for automation that will most benefit from that effort.

Another key advantage is that because you can see the entire test suite, you can find opportunities for reuse.

And, as you think about automating your scripts, you can develop a set of tools or subroutines to use throughout the suite.

In thinking about automation, we should realize that this really is a much broader subject than most people think. Most people think test automation means writing and executing scripts to exercise the article under test. But you can do so much more with automation.

To my way of thinking, one of the most important forms of test automation is the class of tool called *test managers*. A good test management tool enables you to manage your entire test suite, whether the test cases are automated or manual, which is really what we need to do. We need to look at it for totality of what is going on in the article under test, regardless of the method chosen to test. There are several good test management tools on the market. I recommend looking into them.

Here is the point: all testing starts from test design and test case design. You have got to know what you are testing before you start testing!

Test Management

So, where are we? We have designed our test suite and prepared our test cases. It is now time to actually test. By that I mean it is time to execute the test cases and report the results. There are two topics to discuss here: test status and defect management. We will take them in turn.

Test Status

For those of you who have not been to manager school, I will let you in on Lesson 1—the Manager Question. Managers are taught this at the very start. At any time of the day, he or she will come up to you and ask, "How's it going?" If you are not tracking your status, there is only one possible answer: fine.

Of course, if it is not fine, you will wind up at some point later in the project surprising your manager with bad news. This, in some settings, can be considered career limiting behavior! Let's try it a different way.

Most people track the status of their tests with a simple pass/fail. But there is so much more information to be had. Every day, every test case is in a specific state. Let's run through them.

- If you are able to run the test case, its state is <u>ready to run</u>. At the start of the test run, the test engineer (or an automated tool) selects those test cases in the ready state and submits them for execution.

- After the test case has actually run, it will be in one of several states.

  o <u>The test case is being analyzed</u>. We are not yet ready to declare success or failure, or perhaps it failed, but we have not yet completed the analysis necessary for the defect report.

  o <u>The test case was successful</u>. Okay, let's not quibble about this one! I have known testers who want to say that a successful test case is one that finds a bug. PLEASE DON'T DO THAT! First, it is counterintuitive and confusing. Second, it is dangerously close to *schadenfreude*—joy in someone else's problems. Third, it makes a statement that testers and developers compete instead of cooperate. Again, please don't do that. The definition of a successful test case is simple: the test case functioned in accordance with the requirements.

  o <u>The test case failed</u>. This is just what you would expect after my rant above. This test case found a bug. Part of this status is the defect report number. After the fix is delivered, the status changes to <u>ready to run</u>.

- You may not be able to run all the test cases. There are several reasons why this might be true.

  - o The test case not complete. The test case is not finished. Either the test case specification is not complete or the script is not yet ready to go.

  - o The code is not ready. The section of the article under test that the test case examines has not yet been turned over to the test group.

  - o Both of the above. The code is not ready, and the test case has not been completed.

  - o The environment is not available. Some test cases are intended for specific environments. If the intended environment is not available, the test case cannot run.

  - o The test case cannot run until the fix is delivered for a known defect. In this situation, it is important to note the identifier of the defect report.

  - o Once the fix has been delivered, the status changes. Usually, the new status is ready to run.

In the spreadsheets I use to track status, I use simple codes.

R	Ready to run
XC	Not Ready—the code has not been delivered to test
XT	Not Ready—the test case is not written
XB	Not Ready—neither the code nor the test case is ready
A	Executed—in analysis; we don't yet know if it was successful
S	Executed—successful
F (#)	Executed—failed (include defect number)
E	Not run—being held for environment or configuration
H (#)	Not run—being held for a fix to a defect (include defect number)

Table 2 Test case status codes

The status changes on a daily basis and you can use this information to perform a trend analysis. There two very good reasons for tracking status. One reason is to know where you are standing. The other is to know where you are going and when you will get there.

First, an observation: if you draw a chart of successful test cases over time, you will learn something interesting. If the test execution has been planned so that the test cases run are a good distribution of the test suite, you will usually see an S-curve.

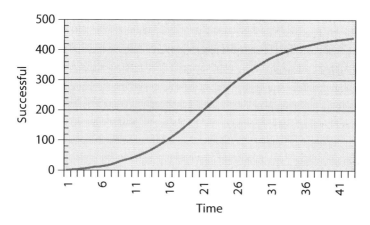

Figure 42: Typical S-Curve

Practically every test I have ever seen follows this pattern. Let's put this observation to use.

Since the S-curve is symmetrical, we can predict the end based on the results at the start.

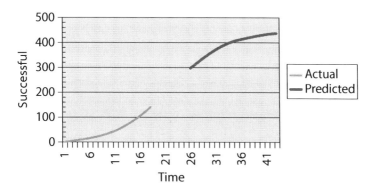

Figure 43: S-Curve (2)

We know what the end points are. How? First, we have just figured out how many test cases are needed. That's what the Behavioral Modeling is all about. Second, we know the end date because, in all likelihood, they told us!

But what if things are not going as smoothly as we hope? In this next chart, if we just look at the actual results, things appear to be getting better.

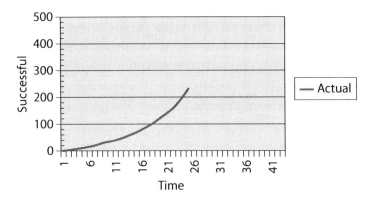

Figure 44: S-Curve (3)

But are things REALLY getting better? Let's add in the predicted results and see.

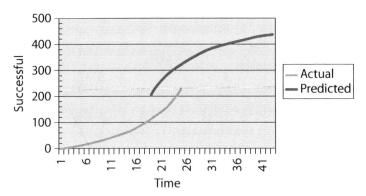

Figure 45: S-Curve (4)

Oops! This tells us very clearly that we will NOT make the end date! This falls into that large grouping I call "bad news, good information."

Now what? As I see it, there are four and only four possible things to do.

1   Add more people. This might help. The trouble is, it might not, and you really won't know until it's too late. Look at it this way: setting many pots of water to boil won't get you your boiling water any faster.

2   Reduce functionality. This might help. The trouble is, if the defects you are finding are evenly distributed, deciding which function to drop won't be easy. If there is a defect-prone region and you don't really need it in the upcoming release, then you can drop it. If you do this, you will have to remove the test cases that cover this function and redraw the chart with the new test suite.

3   Change the end date. This might help. The trouble is, you may not have that luxury. The good news is that if you do decide to change the end date, you can now very accurately predict the new date. Your prediction will be based not on someone's hopes and dreams, but on the operational characteristics of the test itself. And it is easy. Just look at the curve and move out the "predicted" portion until the curve looks smooth. Then all you need to do is read the new end date from the x-axis.

4   There is a fourth option. It is **not** one I recommend, but I will mention it only to be complete: ship it anyway and hope no one notices. They **will** notice, I assure you.

Defect Management

In this section, I want to discuss just a few aspects of defect management, not the entire process. The reason is that I want to concentrate on those aspects of defect management that have gone so horribly wrong at most places. Before we get to the details, consider this a warning: some people consider this approach a bit controversial. (I prefer the term revolutionary.)

Severity No

There are some problems with the severity evaluation of defects as this term is typically used. For one thing, the notions are subjective. Consider this list of severities currently in use at a variety of companies:

- Urgent
- Critical
- Showstopper
- High
- Medium
- Low
- 1
- 2
- 3
- Major
- Minor

I even know of one large company where they ALL are in use, just not in the same divisions. The potential for inconsistency is quite high. The possibility of comparison between projects is quite low.

In addition to the subjective nature of the severity evaluations, a common occurrence is "severity inflation" as projects progress, followed by a sudden "severity deflation" as the scheduled end date approaches.

What is needed is a consistent, easily-understood, inflation-proof system.

Scope Yes

Instead of the subjective terms listed above, defects should be evaluated by the scope of impact they have on the continuation of the test. Given good, systematic test design by a process such as Behavioral Modeling, for example, the impact on the test will be a good analog to the impact on the production system.

Scope	Impact
Application	The entire application or article under test is affected. Either continued testing is impossible, or it is known that the fix will require such pervasive changes that any testing will have to be redone anyway. Testing is halted.
Function	A major function of the article under test is affected. Testing is halted in this function. Testing continues in the other functions.
Feature	A feature of the identified function is affected. Testing is halted in this feature. Testing continues in other features and functions.
Test Case	The identified test case has discovered a defect. This test case cannot be executed until the defect if fixed. Testing continues.
No Impact	The defect does not prevent any testing activity. The most common example of this would be a spelling error on a displayed screen.

Table 3: Scope of impact

Defect Report States

A defect report may be considered to be in a "state" The states identify where the report is in the process workflow.

State	Description	Resposible Party
New	The defect report has been written. It is not yet assigned to anyone for analysis.	Anyone who identifies a problem.
Assigned	The defect report has been assigned to a team member for analysis.	Typically a software engineer on the development team. This may be assigned by the team lead or the software engineer may self assign.
Responded	The assigned team member has responded to the defect report. The possible responses are discussed in Table 5: Defect report responses.	The assignee.
Closed	The response has been accepted and the defect report is closed. This may mean that a repair has been successfully tested.	An authorized member of the test team. The assignee can never close a defect report.
Hold	The defect report is on hold, awaiting some triggering event. There may be several types of holds. For example, the developer may be waiting for more information or the tester may be waiting for the next build.	Varies.

Table 4: Defect report states

Defect Report Responses

A response to a defect report must include a response type.

Response	Description	Comment
Error	A defect exists in the article under test.	A secondary field is used to indicate To Be Fixed or Not To Be Fixed.
Documentation	A defect exists in the documentation of the article under test.	A secondary field is used to indicate To Be Fixed or Not To Be Fixed.
External	The defect is external to the article under test. It may be in third-party software or in an application used by the article under test.	A work-around is needed.
Data	The test data are invalid.	In general, the article under test should guard against this and therefore this may in fact be an error.
Configuration	The test environment is improperly built.	The test environment must be repaired.
User Error	The article under test is working properly; the user made a mistake.	In general, the article under test should guard against this and therefore this may in fact be an error.
Test Case Error	The article under test is working properly; the test case incorrectly reported a failure.	The test case must be repaired.

Not Reproducible	The problem no longer occurs.	There may have been a defect that was repaired by a fix to a different defect, or the circumstances are too complex to achieve consistent results.
Duplicate	This defect has already been reported.	A secondary field must contain the id of the duplicated defect.
Suggestion	This is a request for a modification to the article under test.	A secondary field is used to indicate To Be Fixed or Not To Be Fixed. The change control process must be invoked for modification requests.

Table 5: Defect report responses

Appendix A – Behavioral Model Glossary

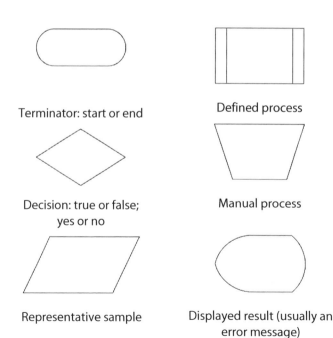

Terminator: start or end

Defined process

Decision: true or false;
yes or no

Manual process

Representative sample

Displayed result (usually an
error message)

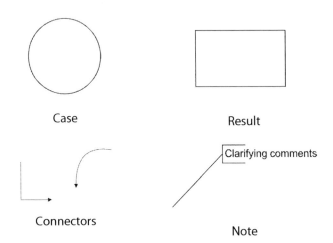

Case

Result

Connectors

Clarifying comments

Note

Appendix B – Tips

As we go through the process of functional decomposition, always look for opportunities to break things down. We are after the simplest representation of the behavior. This results in the least number of tests. Furthermore, by decomposing into the simplest building blocks, the resultant model is easy to understand. This is a good thing! Yes, it is possible to break things down too far. Judgment is required here to get the proper balance.

⌘ ⌘ ⌘

The "defined process" block shows up in all the levels of the model before the lowest level. Remember that this block should be the only block on the path. Otherwise, we indicate that we want to multiply the number of test cases, not add them.

⌘ ⌘ ⌘

Some constructs show up frequently in test design, and there are usually simple ways of handling them. In this section, I will show a few of them. You can create a library for these and just copy and paste into your models, making, of course the required editorial changes.

Consider the situation where the software under test has a command line interface. Most often, command line interfaces allow the user to enter several parameters. These parameters must be validated, and, if any of them are incorrect, some action must be taken.

There are two common ways in which the parsing and analysis take place. In the first of these, the software goes through the list, one at a time, checking as it goes. As soon as the software discovers an invalid parameter, it exits, giving an error message. For Unix programs, this error message is simply a display of the information that describes the usage of the command line.

A slightly more helpful program would issue a message that identifies the specific parameter in error and explains the problem.

Another approach, far more user-friendly, would scan the entire line and give the user information about all the errors at one time rather than requiring the user to reissue the command line as many time as there are erroneous parameters.

The figures on the following pages show how each of these situations is handled in their respective behavior models.

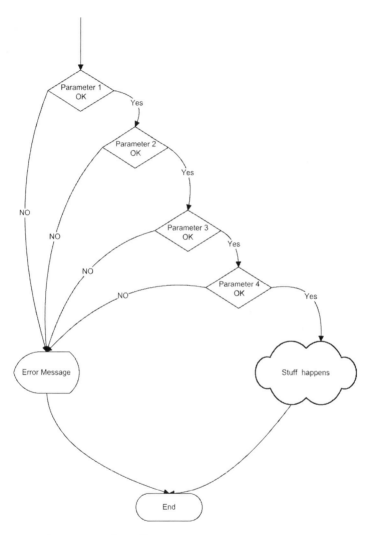

Figure 46: Exit on first error; common error message

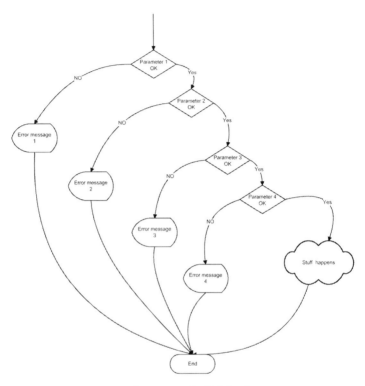

Figure 47: Exit on first error; individual error messages

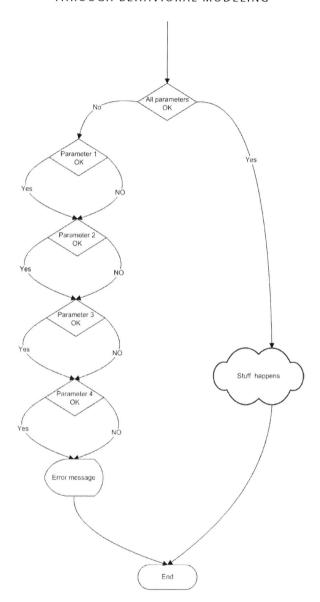

Figure 48: Single-pass scan of input line

Another common situation occurs when the program must handle a multiple choice followed by another multiple choice where these are independent of each other. For example, the program under test must be able to do any of several things and must do all of these on several operating systems. The model would be a case block followed by another case block.

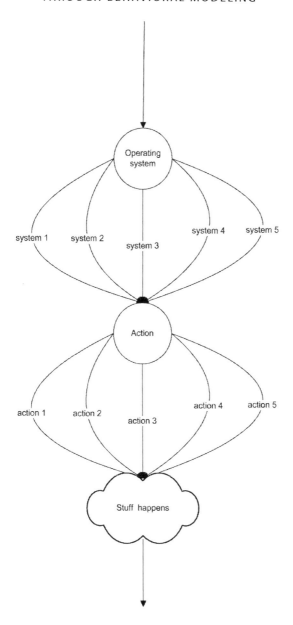

Figure 49: Case after case

Appendix C – *FAST* Test Case Design

TCD ID:	F		
Description:	**FAST**		
Author:	**Shel Prince**		
Original Release:	**1.0**	Date:	**9/7/20xx**

Function:	TCD:	Page:
Balance	FB	
Deposit	FD	
Exceptions	FE	
Sign on	FS	
Transfer	FT	
Withdraw	FW	
String	FR	

Matrix ID:	FB							
Description:	FAST Balance							
Author:	Shel Prince							
Original Release:	1.0		Date: 9/6/20xx					
Test case:	FB01	FB02	FB03	FB04	FB05	FB06	FB07	FB08
Control Points:								
To Account:	*	*	*	*	*	*		
Checking	*		*	*				
Savings		*			*	*		
Account exists?	N	Y	Y	N	Y	Y	Y	Y
Current Balance:			*	*	*	*	*	*
Zero			*		*			
non-zero				*		*	*	*
maximum amount				*		*	*	
0.01					*			*
Expected Results	"Requested account does not exist.		Correct bslsnce displayed.					

Matrix ID:	FD					
Description:	FAST Deposit					
Author:	Shel Prince					
Original Release:	1.0		Date: 9/6/20xx			
Test case:	FD01	FD02	FD03	FD04	FD05	FD06
Control Points:						
To Account:	*	*	*	*	*	*
Checking	*	*	*			
Savings				*	*	*
Account exists?	N	Y	Y	N	Y	Y
Amount of deposit:		*	*		*	*
valid			*			*
invalid		*			*	
Expected Results	"Requested account does not exist. Re-enter."	"Invalid amount. Re-enter." Re-entered amount accepted.	Account balance updated with the deposited amount.	"Requested Account Does Not Exist. Re-enter."	"Invalid amount. Re-enter."	Account balance updated with the deposited amount.

Matrix ID:	FE						
Description:	Fast Exceptions						
Author:	Shel Prince						
Original Release:	1.0		Date: 9/6/20xx				
Test case:	FE01	FE02	FE03	FE04	FE05	FE06	FE07
Control Points:							
Cancel during:	*	*	*	*	*	*	
Balance	*		*	*			
Deposit		*			*	*	
Site-on	N	Y	Y	N	Y	Y	Y
transfer			*	*	*	*	*
withdraw			*		*		
non-zero				*		*	*
Out of paper				*		*	*
FAST Out of cash					*		
Expected Results	Transaction canceled display returns to menu.			"This machine is temporarily out of service."			

Matrix ID:	FW									
Description:	FAST Withdraw									
Author:	Shel Prince									
Original Release:	1.0		Date: 9/6/20xx							

Test case:	FW01	FW02	FW03	FW04	FW05	FW06	FW07	FW08	FW09	FW10
Control Points:										
From Account:	*	*	*	*	*	*	*	*	*	*
Checking	*		*	*	*	*				
Savings		*					*	*	*	*
From Account exists?	N	N	Y	Y	Y	Y	Y	Y	Y	Y
Amount of withdrawal:			*	*	*	*	*	*	*	*
zero			*				*			
more than in "from"				*				*		
Multiple of $20?					Y	Y			Y	Y
More than in FAST?					Y	N			Y	N
Expected Results	"From Account Does Not Exist"		"Cannot withdraw zero."	"Insufficient funds in From Account. Re-enter or cancel."	"Not enough cash to service your request. Re-enter or cancel."	Cash dispensed. Amount deducted from account.	"Cannot withdraw zero."	"Insufficient funds in From Account. Re-enter or cancel."	"Not enough cash to service your request. Re-enter or cancel."	Cash dispensed. Amount deducted from account.

Appendix D – Verification

INTRODUCTION

While it is not the intention of this book to go into depth on the subject of verification, it is a very important topic. In this appendix, we will have a short overview of the process. I sometimes call this process "Testing Without Testing."

Most of the time, when we say "testing" we mean something like "running the thing." So, how do we test without running the thing? How do we test without testing?

Let's take a closer look at our definition. The purpose of testing is to finds bugs, right? So if we expand our definition to include any activity intended to find bugs, then we go beyond just running the thing. We can include reviewing in our testing definition. Execution-based testing is called *validation*, while non-execution-based testing is called *verification*.

Can we review code instead of executing it? Yes. Of course, most of our software is pretty complex, so reviewing it may not be all that efficient, but it is certainly worth a try.

Then is reviewing code the best use of our time? That depends. It depends on where the bugs are that we are trying to find. Interestingly, industry averages tell us that 70–80 percent of the defects are actually in the specification and design. So, if we can review things like requirements, specifications, designs, and the like, we can prevent possibly 75 percent or more of the defects before we even begin the "testing."

One of the problems with this, though, is that most people say, "We don't have time for all that stuff." This is a reasonable gut reaction, but the numbers don't bear this out. Actually, every time someone has tried to measure the resource and schedule impact of verification, they get the same result: **Projects are faster and cheaper if you do verification than if you don't.**

There are a variety of terms to describe the process. Most commonly, we call this *peer review* or *technical review*. I will use the general term, verification, in the section that follows.

There are several levels of formality that may be used. I'll discuss an overview of the most formal level; you can tailor this for your own needs. Consider the complexity of the work product, the risk if the final product fails, and the maturity of the organization and its tolerance for process. (Yes, I know that there is a huge difference between process and procedures, but let's not go into that!)

Let's look at the basics.

Verification is a process designed to identify—and thus eliminate—defects in all manner of work products. Examples of these work products include requirements, functional specifications, test plans, source code, user interface layouts, and others. The basic concept is that an ad hoc team comes together for the purpose of reviewing a work product. The process is a tool to be used by the author of the work product to be assured that it is as complete, clear, and correct as possible.

The members of the review team each play a specific assigned role. The roles are:

Author. This role is self-assigned. This person is the one who created the work product in the first place.

Moderator. This person has the responsibility to manage the entire review, and keep the meeting from devolving into either a design session or a free-for-all! Not everybody wants to do this, and not everybody who wants to is ideally suited for the role.

Recorder. This person takes the notes. This should NOT be the author or moderator.

Reviewers. These are the folks who do the actual content review and present their findings.

[Observer]. This is an optional addition to the team. The observer is usually there to learn how the process works so he or she can be prepared to take an active role in the future. I usually qualify this by saying that observers must have the moderator's permission to attend. Their role is to, as the name implies, observe, and not participate.

[Subject Matter Expert]. Sometimes it helps to have an additional member of the team who can clarify the matter at hand and may also be able to help describe what is technically feasible.

There may be some overlap among the roles. For example, the Moderator and the Subject Matter Expert may also be Reviewers. Note that for the Author, there is no overlap: the Author cannot fill any of the other roles.

There are eight steps in the process, as follows:

- Planning
- Kick-off
- Individual Review
- Collation / Discussion Preparation
- Discussion
- Defect Logging
- Revision / Confirmation
- Final Report

These steps will be discussed more fully in the next section. For now, the following table shows who is involved at each of the steps.

	Plan	Kick-off	Individual Review	Collation	Discussion	Defect Logging	Revision, Confirmation	Final Report
Author	√	√	(√)	(√)	√		√	(√)
Moderator	√	√	(√)	√	√	(√)	(√)	√
Recorder		√			√	√		
Reviewers		√	√		√		√	

Table 6: Roles and Responsibilities

Steps

PLANNING

Role	Action
Author	Selects/requests a Moderator
	Assists Moderator in his/her tasks
Moderator	Assigns roles
	Creates review package
	Schedules meetings

When an author determines that his or her work product is ready for review, he or she must first get someone to serve as moderator. The moderator functions as an overall coordinator of the review activities. In the planning stage, the moderator first assesses the readiness of the work product for review. "Readiness" means there is a high likelihood of successful completion of the review. If the moderator determines that there are too many defects in the work product, for example, he or she may deem that the work product is not ready and suggest that the author clean it up before submitting the work product for verification

Assuming readiness, the moderator selects individuals for the review team and assigns them their roles. The people chosen should represent the various stakeholders. Since almost all work products are responses to predecessor work products, one or more of the team members could be people who were responsible for the predecessor. Since almost all work products are the drivers for follow-on work, some of the team members could be people who must perform the next step or steps.

For example, consider the case of a functional requirements document. This is often the response to a marketing requirements document, and therefore one member of the review team could be the author of the marketing requirements document. This allows for assurance that the functional requirements correctly interpret the marketing requirements. Similarly, the functional requirements document is input to the functional specification and the test plan, so team members could include both the person who will be creating the functional requirements document and the person who will be creating the test plan.

Generally, one should avoid having as a team member any manager who has his or her own employees on the review team. It is occasionally necessary to ignore this rule, but one should do so with caution. Some people are less comfortable in this situation than others.

The ideal size is five to nine people.

The review package consists of the work product, any predecessor documents, and the standard for the type of article. The package may be hard copy, soft copy, or merely pointers to where the information exists.

KICK-OFF

Role	Action
Moderator	Distributes review package Conducts meeting Secures commitments
Author	Presents high-level overview of the item(s) to be reviewed
Reviewers	Listen, learn Ask questions
Recorder	Log duration of the meeting Log list of attendees

At the kick-off meeting, the team gets information about the work product. If the review package is hard copy, it is distributed at this meeting. Since the team may be scattered across several locations, the material must be available for all team members at this time.

The kick-off meeting is intended to be quite brief. It generally lasts no more than thirty minutes. At the meeting, the author will give a brief summary of the article and may alert the team to areas of concern. It may also happen that some areas of the article are not completed, and so the author would point this out. Those areas may be subject for review at a later date.

In order for the reviewers to have sufficient time for their individual reviews, the kick-off should be at least five working days prior to the discussion. This allows the reviewers the flexibility to weave their preparation around their primary assignments. As an alternative, the team may decide how long they need and schedule the discussion as a result of that decision at the kick-off.

If any reviewers feel that they cannot complete the individual review in the allotted time, this is their opportunity to either opt for replacement or suggest a different date for the discussion.

The moderator should remind the team members of the purpose of the technical review. The purpose is to develop findings for the work product, not to redesign the article.

The recorder's function here is to log the number of attendees and the duration of the meeting. This information will be useful later when we are calculating the return on investment of the process.

Note that the kick-off meeting does not necessarily need to be a face-to-face gathering. In fact, it may be that team members are in different locations. Consider conference calls and video hook-ups. In some circumstances, e-mail might also be considered as an alternative. There are some disadvantages to this, but it may occasionally be necessary.

INDIVIDUAL REVIEW

Role	Action
Reviewers	Review the article Record findings Transmit findings to Moderator before the Discussion
Moderator	Monitors Reviewers' progress Helps Reviewers with process issues
Author	Answers questions from the Reviewers

During this step, the reviewers perform their individual review, gathering their findings. The findings belong in one of the following categories:

- Defects

- Questions

- External issues

- Praise

The reason for using discrete categories is that it helps assure that the review does not devolve into a re-design exercise. The category list may be upgraded or modified from time to time, but not on a product-by-product basis. This will allow for project comparisons and statistical analyses.

Defects. The defects fall into one of five types. The types are:

Error – a statement is incorrect.

Conflict – a statement is in disagreement with a different statement in the work product.

Missing – some necessary or required information is not present.

Extra – some feature or design has been added that is not accounted for in the predecessor document. For example, if there is no requirement for a particular product to run on some platform, then having specification or design to support that platform would be a defect of type "extra."

Unclear – a statement in the work product has several possible interpretations or is written in a way that could confuse the user of the article.

It should be noted that the defects identified during Individual Review are not recorded in the incident management database at this time. That action occurs after the discussion, once consensus has been reached that the finding is, in fact, a defect.

Questions. Some findings are questions to be asked of either the author or subject matter expert. Generally, these are requests for background information or information that is nominally outside the area of the work product. One word of caution: if a reviewer has a question, it may be that something is missing or unclear. Either of these situations would be a defect, not a question.

External Issues. Sometimes, reviewers uncover difficulties that are relevant to the use of the product being developed but not under the control of the team doing the developing. For example, if a specification calls for use of a third party application, a potential external issue could concern run-time licenses for that application.

Praise. It is useful to take note of things that are done especially well in the work product so that others may learn. Besides, many authors feel a bit sensitive about having their worked scrutinized, and it's nice to complement them. Of course, the goal is to conduct the reviews in such a way that no one feels picked on, but as the process is introduced, there may be a bit of trepidation.

The reviewers transmit their findings to the moderator the day before the discussion. Any errors of the nature of typos, grammatical errors, spelling errors, and the like should be sent separately from the findings. These will be handed over to the author and not covered in the meeting. (Some people just like to use marked-up copies of the article for this purpose.)

COLLATION

Role	Action
Moderator	Gathers findings Prepares agenda
Author	Assists Moderator

The moderator collects the findings and prepares the agenda for the meeting. Most moderators choose to handle the findings in page sequence rather than skipping all around in the work product. Occasionally, there may be reasons for placing a particularly serious problem first regardless of its location.

If there are very many defects being reported, the Moderator should consider canceling the review since the work product may not be quite ready. In this situation, the findings should be given to the author for use in updating the article. A review can then be rescheduled.

DISCUSSION

Role	Action
Moderator	Keeps discussion focused on identification, not solution Keeps discussion focuses on the work product, not the author
Reviewers	Present their findings Participate in determining Review result
Recorder	Logs prep time for each reviewer Finalizes the findings log Summarizes findings at end of discussion Logs duration, attendees
Author	Listens, learns Answers questions if asked Thanks the reviewers for their help
Observer	Observes
Manager	Stays away

A suggested agenda is:

Moderator distributes copies of agenda and collation report to reviewers.

Moderator describes purpose of meeting, process, and ground rules.

Moderator polls reviewers, asking how much time they spent in their preparation. If any of the reviewers are not prepared, they should change role from reviewer to observer if they wish to remain. If too many reviewers are not prepared, the meeting should be cancelled and rescheduled for another time.

Moderator polls reviewers for any general comments before beginning a point-by-point review. This may include general praise or comments about missing items that cannot be pegged to a particular location in the work product.

Each of the identified findings is presented in sequence. If any of the findings is a question, the team decides if this indicates a defect or not. If it is not a defect, the author answers the question. For findings of type "defect," consensus is reached on the severity and type.

Group searches for new defects. These would be findings not previously reported. Typically, the earlier discussion my trigger observations in the team that no one individual had reported.

Recorder notes any new findings as well as changes to the previously identified findings. This includes the description, severity, and type. The severities are:

1 – The end product would be unusable if this were not fixed.

2 – A major function of the end product would be unusable if this were not fixed.

3 –A feature (part of a function) of the end product would be unusable if this were not fixed.

4 –A particular situation would cause a failure in the end product if this were not fixed.

5 – This would not necessarily result in an observable failure in the end product, but it could potentially cause some difficulty or annoyance.

Recorder reads the list of findings. This gives the person who reported it a chance to add clarification if necessary, and gives the author a chance to ask any final questions about it. It also gives the team a chance to hear the entire list, which is useful in forming an over-all impression. This helps with the determination of the discussion outcome.

Team determines the outcome. There are four possible outcomes:

Accept as is. No changes are necessary.

Accept with changes. Author makes the changes based on the findings. No confirmation is necessary.

Revise with informal confirmation. Author makes changes based on the findings. The changes are informally confirmed.

Revise and hold another Formal Review. The findings are significant enough that the team decides that another Formal Review is needed after the author has made the changes.

If the outcome was "Revise with informal confirmation," the team decides on the confirmation technique(s) as well as assigns individuals to the confirmation as appropriate. Examples of informal confirmation techniques are:

- One person from the review team confirms (no meeting)

- Several people from the team confirm (no meeting)

- Author presents changes to team (meeting)

Author collects any marked packages that may contain the typos, and so forth, if they have not been previously transmitted.

Author thanks the team members.

The discussion should last no more than two hours. It is sometimes necessary to divide an article into sections to achieve this goal. Rarely, an article is long, complex, and cannot be divided. In this case, the meeting may have to exceed the two-hour limit.

DEFECT LOGGING

Role	Action
Recorder	Logs defects to the incident management database

Following the discussion, the recorder enters the defects into the incident management system. This is not the onerous chore it may seem to be for two reasons. First, since most of them will have been transmitted electronically, there can be a lot of cut-and-paste. Second, the expectation is that the number of defects found will not be prohibitive, or the discussion would not have taken place. As an alternative, some review teams may choose to use a less formal method of tracking the defects, such as a spreadsheet. *(On the other hand, if you are going to copy the information to a spreadsheet, why not just go ahead and copy it to the incident manager so you can take advantage of the tools available?)*

REVISION, CONFIRMATION

Role	Action
Author	Revises the work product as indicated by the Review findings
Moderator	Monitors revision progress Assures all revisions have been made
Reviewers`	Confirm revisions as assigned during the Discussion

FINAL REPORT

Role	Action
Moderator	Summarizes the verification Performs statistical analysis as needed Makes recommendations as appropriate

The statistical analysis addresses issues such as number of findings of each type and how much time on average was spent per finding.